"Joe Mulvaney is one of the most prophetic voices in Ireland today. *Speak Out For Reform* shares his personal story of priestly ministry and advocacy for genuine reform that could transform outdated man-made rules and patriarchal structures. He offers a vision of an inclusive Church that embraces everyone and reflects the hospitality at the heart of Celtic spirituality"
Bishop Bridget Mary Meehan, Sarasota, Florida

"You have deepened my understanding of the many needs in the Church that we should be advocating such as women's rights, democracy and the need to rid the Church of clericalism. The lay people need to be involved in decision making and the selection of bishops."
Dorine Groome, Kinnegad, County Westmeath.

"This is a must have book. It is a compelling account of his journey in life, leading to a valuable critique of the clerical church and a brave vision of what the Church could be if we could only wrestle it from the hands of career clerics".
Fr. Brian Darcy,--Sunday World-February 10th, 2019.

"It is a courageous and very insightful book, full of hard-won practical wisdom by way of Church reform that is so desperately needed. I never found a line that I didn't agree with – and that's unusual for this academic"
Thomas Groome, Prof. Theology & Religious Education, Boston College

SPEAK

OUT

FOR REFORM

IN THE CATHOLIC CHURCH

A CALL TO ACTION

Joe Mulvaney

Buy Online:

www.wearechurchireland.ie//last-supper

www.eprint.ie

Contact:

speakoutforreform@gmail.com

ISBN: 978-1-9164349-2-9

Printed and bound in Ireland by eprint limited www.eprint.ie

You will learn the truth, and the truth will make you free.

John (8:32)

Happy are those who hunger and thirst for what is right;
They shall be satisfied.

Matthew (5:6)

In fide, unitas;   In core faith, unity;
In dubiis, libertas;   In debatable matters, liberty;
In omnibus, caritas.   In all things, love.

Attributed to St Augustine of Hippo

So, stand your ground, with truth buckled around your waist
and integrity for a breastplate,
wearing for shoes on your feet
the eagerness to spread the gospel of peace
and always carrying the shield of faith.

Ephesians (6: 14-16)

But what is needed now is people-power. We need to join hands and hearts to work together for a reformed, renewed Church. We the people must make it happen. We need to take steps to change the up-down, pyramid model of church to a more circular model – a community of equals – each with different gifts, all working to build up the Body of Christ. We are companions on the journey, partners in ministry, and we need to build together a more accountable, caring pastoral church.

Bishop Bridget Mary Meehan
Association of Roman Catholic Women Priests

For all those followers of Jesus Christ
who cherish the Good News of Love
and who favour
reform in the Roman Catholic Church
as well as
reunion of all Christian Churches.

CONTENTS

PART 4 – SPEAK OUT LETTERS

ACKNOWLEDGEMENTS

I wish to thank my wife, Maureen Leonard, for her loving support and encouragement in the production of this book. I have been preoccupied with this project since January 2017. Accordingly, I am deeply grateful to her for her patience and advice. In my times of struggle with this book, her wisdom assured me of the value of our joint vision and the potential of Catholic people speaking out. Our vision is of the immense good to be harnessed if the 1.2bn Roman Catholic Church was to announce repentance for the sins of sexism and misogyny and a new beginning to involve equality, justice and ordination of women.

Our three sons also deserve thanks for their help with the project. I wish to thank Brendan for his typing skill, patience and editorial advice over eighteen months of hard work on multiple drafts. Thanks is also due to Eamon for his publishing expertise and wonderful computer skills in preparation of all drafts. Finally, a special thank you to Cathal who continued to challenge me to pursue church reform and produce some kind of text or credo that might make sense to his generation. Thanks also to extended family members for their comments and support. I also called on the expertise of Maureen's nephew, Conor Doherty, who is a professional photographer in Sligo.

The author David Rice deserves thanks for his book *Shattered Vows* and his work in setting up the support group *Leaven* in 1986 for former clerics and religious. He helped to nurture the original idea for this book and I availed of the professional expertise in his *Killaloe Hedge-School for Writers* some years ago.

The members of the reform group *We Are Church Ireland* within which I am active have also provided much inspiration and support. I marvel at their endurance and hard work against injustices in the Catholic Church. I wish to thank Colm Holmes, Phil Dunne,

Tony MacCarthaigh, Gina Menzies, Ursula Halligan and Mary McAleese for their reading of initial drafts and their useful suggestions. My special gratitude to the author and theologian Angela Hanley, from Athlone, for her extensive editorial work. She was tough but fair in her judgements and suggestions. My failure to implement all of her editorial recommendations mean that deficiencies in the final text are totally my fault. I also wish to thank fellow Coolaney writer and poet, Micheál Farry, who now resides in Trim. He devoted much time to the proof reading task and suggested many corrections.

I wish to acknowledge the competence and advice of Gerry Conlon and his team at eprint. Their help was very important in this self-publishing venture. I wish to especially acknowledge the brilliant cartoons of Sean O'Brien included in this book. I tried to contact the current holder of copyright but without success. These very fitting cartoons provide for levity in the midst of my serious reform viewpoint. Some of the cartoons were published in a book called *Jesus Saves* by Sean O'Brien. It was published by sPearWay Ltd in London in 1997. This was a book for joyful Christians and helped make sense of some Bible texts. I first came across these cartoons about fifteen years ago through our friends Colm Holmes and Soline Humbert of the group *Brothers and Sisters in Christ* (BASIC) which campaigned for the ordination of women. This group merged in 2012 with *We Are Church Ireland*. *BASIC* had an agreement with Sean O'Brien for use of his cartoons as fund-raising postcards. I tried to locate contact details for Sean O'Brien or sPearWay Ltd as per the data provided in the *Jesus Saves* book, but received no response. My book is not being published for commercial gain. Any proceeds will be given to the Society of St Vincent de Paul. Accordingly, although I would have preferred to do so with formal permission, I have proceeded to include the cartoons in this book for the enjoyment of readers. I am willing to speak with the person now holding the copyright to the cartoons if they wish to contact me.

FOREWORD

LETTER OF HIS HOLINESS POPE FRANCIS TO THE PEOPLE OF GOD
(Excerpts)

"With shame and repentance, we acknowledge as an ecclesial community that we were not where we should have been, that we did not act in a timely manner, realizing the magnitude and the gravity of the damage done to so many lives. We showed no care for the little ones; we abandoned them."

"The extent and the gravity of all that has happened requires coming to grips with this reality in a comprehensive and communal way."

"Every one of the baptized should feel involved in the ecclesial and social change that we so greatly need."

"Without the active participation of all the Church's members, everything being done to uproot the culture of abuse in our communities will not be successful in generating the necessary dynamics for sound and realistic change."

"To say 'no' to abuse is to say an emphatic 'no' to all forms of clericalism."

Vatican City, 20 August 2018

The full text of this historic letter was published in the Irish Times on 21 August 2018 shortly before the Pope arrived in Ireland. The context of the letter was the Grand Jury Report from Pennsylvania and ongoing reports of abuse from all over the globe. The letter was a disappointment for some people. However, despite shortcomings, I believe that the document is very important and gives us much material to discuss. Unlike Catholics in the past who refused to believe victims, Pope Francis admits the magnitude of the problem. He also spoke during his visit to Ireland of "attitudes of aloofness and clericalism that at times in your history have given the real image of an authoritarian, harsh and autocratic church."

There is a danger now that innocent Catholics are being implicated in the abuse by their silence and deference to clergy.

Abuse continues to happen and cannot be dismissed as something that happened in the past. A clerical meaning system, culture or ethos that is intrinsically disordered will inevitably produce wrongdoing. It appears to me that Catholic clericalism is centred around an elite caste or religious hierarchy of celibate males who claim special knowledge, privilege and power.

However, the historic nature of this letter – at a time of disillusionment for some Catholics – is that Pope Francis repeatedly states that we must all actively participate with priests and bishops in the breaking down of clericalism and the massive task of urgent reform. I presume this means that women and men must share in teaching, service, ordained ministry and governance. If all this happens over the coming years, then it could usher in a new Catholic Church era of truth, justice and love.

INTRODUCTION

On 14 June 1970, a beautiful sunny day, thirty of us young men were ordained as priests at All Hallows College, Drumcondra, Dublin to provide ministry to people in America, Canada, Australia, England and South Africa. A class picture was taken in front of the main door of the seminary. We were sent forth from under the following motto which remains carved over that main door:

Euntes Docete Omnes Gentes – Go, Make Disciples of All Nations

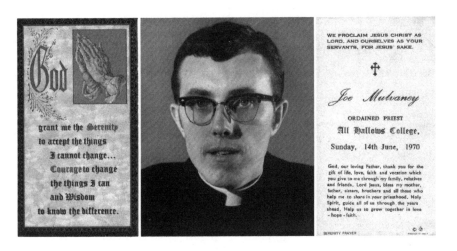

My ordination card stated that we were going out to proclaim the Good News of Jesus Christ. Jesus announced that we are all special sons and daughters of a loving God. His message is that reality is gracious, all will be delivered from evil and all will be well. Jesus Christ as Risen Lord, is with us and assures us that life is changed and not ended at death. The Holy Spirit of God inspires our response of joy, thanksgiving, love for all and action for justice within a community of believers. Thankfully, my faith in that gospel message remains unchanged. That core Catholic faith sustained my ancestors in difficult times and it helps me.

However, nearly fifty years later, much has changed for all of us. The seminary is closed, and All Hallows College is now part of the Dublin City University campus. There is a growing crisis within the Roman Catholic Church in the developed world. The shadow of child abuse haunts us worldwide. All the evidence shows that Canon Laws and official directives about cover-up issued from the Vatican. The bishops were obedient to those instructions and now suffer blame. Pope Francis has admitted that "we showed no care for the little ones." All of this has served to scandalise Catholics providing service and ministries in every parish. Refusal by the hierarchy to listen, share power and reform has led to alienation and disillusionment.

The riches of updated Vatican II (1962-1965) teachings were never fully shared with Catholics worldwide and new structures were not developed. A clerical Catholic ethos which suppresses women, enforces celibacy, extols virginity and denigrates homosexuals repels people today who value the joyful celebration of sexuality and respect women. The teaching of a very small group of male clerics in Rome on artificial contraception in 1968 has not been accepted by the vast majority of Catholic people.

Somewhere in excess of a hundred thousand priests have left the active ministry during the past fifty years seemingly without any high-level review as to the root causes of this serious loss of key personnel. I am one of that number. There is now a severe shortage of priests in the developed world as a result of medieval restrictions by Rome. The tragic result is a needless Eucharistic and pastoral care famine. Accordingly, many Catholics have walked away from parish practice and avoid clerics who assert that there can be no change and reformers should consider joining a Protestant church. Most Catholics have not walked away from Jesus. Catholic people know that there is no shortage of excellent women and men in every parish with the talents to provide reformed ministry, priestly service and leadership. Catholic people are annoyed and insulted at the charade of praying for restricted vocations. However, the bishops seem unable to listen and lead even as Pope Francis encourages them to assess the pastoral needs of their region. A dysfunctional hierarchical system means that the bishops are not engaging properly with priests who feel discouraged as a result. Some Catholic lay people are shocked by the gap which has developed between clerics and themselves on issues such as ordination for women, homophobia, responsible parenthood and power-sharing. People are sickened by the monstrous revelations in our Church over the past fifty years regarding institutional cruelty and injustice. Most Catholic people hold firm to Jesus Christ in faith, hope and prayer. They continue to go about doing good with love in their hearts, but they have lost confidence in some aspects of the Roman Catholic institution and clerical leadership which refuses to listen to the cries of the people for urgent change.

In this book I share my story and Catholic faith journey. Much has changed for me since childhood in rural Sligo in the 1950s and seminary studies from 1963 to 1970. Much has changed for me since ordination and my years as a priest. I now share my experience with you as a married man, parent and practising Catholic who favours updating and change in the Catholic Church. I retain faith in the Good News of Jesus Christ but have come to disagree with clerical teachings on issues such as suppression of women, enforced celibacy, artificial contraception, homophobia and patriarchal refusal to share power. I value personal prayer as well as participation in my local parish and community. I feel empowered to share my story and my viewpoint. I am prepared to work with others for reform in the Catholic Church. I am an active member of a group called *We Are Church Ireland* which is working to end injustices in the Catholic Church. I want all Catholic people to feel empowered and to contribute to the updating and reunion of the Church.

I want to highlight issues in the Catholic Church today and the improvements that are needed. In our ongoing Catholic conversations around the crisis, we need to clarify the meanings and exact usage of certain words such as Church and Church Teaching. Is Church a building or a historical institution? Is it the hierarchy or the People of God? Is Church Teaching the teaching of an elite corps or is it the accepted consensus faith of the whole Catholic community? We also need to differentiate between the fundamental message of Jesus Christ versus non-core clerical rules, structures, rituals, opinions and traditions which may be repealed, reviewed, changed, abandoned or developed over time by the People of God. An example of such non-core teaching is the one relating to artificial contraception which has not been accepted by the People of God. However, the people do agree with the clerics that there is a loving personal God and that life has many dimensions and that the way we should live is by love and action for justice.

Like many others, I am grappling with some issues which confront us as a Catholic Church family today and hereby submit my contribution to the much-needed Catholic conversation in preparation for Vatican III. I am aware that the issues vary considerably depending on different cultures and on the stage of economic, social or religious development of a country. The Church may appear to thrive where there is poverty, superstition, lack of education, fear and underdevelopment. However, it appears to me that our Christian challenge should be to act together with those people for justice, development, education and freedom. The further massive challenge then in the developed world is to present a meaningful religious message and challenging narrative while avoiding anti-modernism. There have been huge developments in Ireland since the Eucharistic Congress in 1932. There was a holy veneer of piety, devotion and subservience at that time. There were plenty of religious and priestly vocations during those decades of primitive development and high unemployment. However, we now know that there was a very dark underbelly to that Catholic society. Thankfully, there has been growth and development. Ireland today is a better place but with much room for improvement.

I acknowledge the limitations of my viewpoint and accept that we need robust dialogue and active listening to all opinions. I am not a theologian, philosopher or biblical scholar. Many of those scholars have produced excellent books about the growing crisis in our Catholic Church over the past decades and I am pleased to recommend some of those books to you in the bibliography. I am presenting a parental and pastoral point of view. I am passionate about the potential for good if the 1.2 billion Roman Catholic Church set out on a new pilgrimage of serious reform and ecumenical endeavour leading towards reunion. I dare to assemble my viewpoint into this book because the issues to do with the priestly calling of all baptised persons, equality and ordination for women, positive celebration of sexuality as well as power sharing/collegiality are of huge importance.

Pope Francis has provided us with a glimmer of hope since 2013. We respect his warm pastoral presence, simple lifestyle and concern for the needy. We welcome his emphasis on joy, mercy, love and care for all of creation. It was wonderful for us as Irish Catholics to welcome him to Ireland for the World Meeting of Families. He provided inspiration for us on our pilgrim way. We recognise the constraints under which he operates and are aware of the entrenched forces of opposition to his program. However, Pope Francis has repeatedly invited our opinions, good sense and suggestions as baptised Catholic people. He did so on numerous occasions leading up to the Synods on the Family in 2014 and 2015. In March 2018, Pope Francis urged young people to get involved, ask questions, challenge old systems and to "make your voice heard, let it resonate in communities and let it be heard by your shepherds of souls." He repeated that message in his address to the assembled bishops at the opening of the Synod in October 2018. It is very important that we respond to his invitation and that we speak our truth openly and honestly to all bishops, priests and the Papal Nuncio.

We all have different insights and useful contributions to make towards a very worthwhile consensus. We, Catholic people, must take a strong stand on behalf of future generations and our local parish communities. Some cardinals and clerics (as distinct from pastoral priests) appear trapped within a medieval mindset. They refuse to consider obvious changes and seem prepared to tolerate Eucharistic and pastoral care famine. They do not appear to have the same concerns as us parents or as settled parishioners who value local community. The bishops are the key pastors in each diocese. We need to speak to them in response to Pope Francis. We must voice our support for Pope Francis in his attempt to implement the Vatican II teaching on collegial cooperation of the bishops with the Pope. We must also show our support for Pope Francis as he encourages us all into a healthy conversation in parish assemblies and diocesan synods. We can let them know clearly the key reforms that are needed from our point of view. This should help to inform their decision-making in Vatican III.

I have written to my bishop, parish priest and Papal Nuncio. Copies of those letters are at the end of this book. You are also invited to do the same on the presumption that you have not lost hope completely in the Catholic Church. You may be a practising Catholic or one of the millions that have walked away. However, you may still believe that there is a treasure for us and our young people obscured behind all the bad news of the last decades. If you agree that serious updating is needed, and that Pope Francis is sincere in asking for our opinions then you are invited to read, respond and join in the action. You have your insights, opinions and a vital contribution to make via letter-writing, open communication and action within small basic Christian communities. Please write to your bishop, parish priest and Papal Nuncio.

The priests are no longer going forth from All Hallows College. However, all of us as followers of Jesus Christ have been given the responsibility through our baptism to go forth and bear witness in our families and communities. People are searching for meaning, purpose, personal value and a 'Higher Power' – a stronghold – in their 21st century lives. I think that reformed religion, personal and family prayer, action for justice, joyful parish liturgies as well as marriage and family enrichment programs can help to light the darkness and be a positive component of healthy lives. We can all help to change the outdated teachings, traditions and structures which repel many adults and young people. Amidst all the gloom and shameful news, this is a project to which all of us can contribute.

This book is not written or published for personal profit. Any profits which may accrue will be given to the Society of St Vincent de Paul. The purpose of this book is to advocate for reform in the Catholic Church based on my experience as priest and parent. You are also invited to speak out and to be the change.

Go, therefore, make disciples of all nations; baptise them in the name of the Father and of the Son and of the Holy Spirit, and teach them to observe all the commands I gave you. And know that I am with you always; yes, to the end of time.
Matthew (28:19-20)

PART 1

PERSONAL STORY

AND

FAITH JOURNEY

1

FROM THE OX MOUNTAINS TO ALL HALLOWS, 1945-1966

**A view of the Mulvaney homestead in the townland of Cabra,
nestled in the Ox mountains near Coolaney, County Sligo**

Away out foreign, there was Holocaust and horror under Hitler. There was poverty and peace in rural Sligo far removed from the theatres of war in November 1943 when Patrick Mulvaney of Cabra married Kathleen Bowie of the same townland in the local Catholic Church of the Sacred Heart and St Joseph at Rockfield in the parish of Killoran. I arrived as their firstborn of seven in March 1945. The awful war was drawing to a close; fifty-five million people had been slaughtered; ten million were displaced; and hundreds of thousands were incinerated in Japan by the atomic bombs. The civil and political leaders had led the world into hell. I was beginning my life journey into a much-changed world. I grew up on a small thirty-acre farm on the southern slopes of the Ox Mountains. All family members had to work hard together in order to eke out a living. The nearest village was three miles away in Coolaney. It was quite an adventure to cycle fifteen miles to the big town of Sligo – no cars in those days except for the doctor, priest, shopkeeper and teacher. It was a traditional Catholic rural area with a sprinkling of Church of Ireland neighbours. In those difficult post war years, with no electricity or running water, simple faith in God was all around us.

The Livingstone family were local Church of Ireland neighbours. Whilst "ecumenical matters" were in deep freeze at clerical level there were cordial and friendly relationships between our two families. Granny Mulvaney acted as midwife and helped deliver Livingstone children. My father and William Livingstone ploughed the fields together with their two horses and helped each other with farm work. William always owned a bull which provided service for all cows regardless of religious persuasion. William taught us how to play the card game 25 during late-night sessions while his wife Frances MacMaster served up tea, scones and jam for us. It was a valuable childhood experience to work and play with Church of Ireland neighbours. In later studies, I was impressed by the honesty of the Church reformers through the centuries and their emphasis on speaking the truth. In general, there were good relationships between Catholics and Protestants in our area. We grew up to respect and cooperate with each other. We came to understand that we were all disciples of Jesus and that love of God and fellow human beings superseded all outdated sectarian division. Life was tough, and all were struggling to make a living from mixed farming on the mountains. Sometimes, mother and father danced around the concrete kitchen floor with us in their arms as we listened to traditional Irish music and songs on the old gramophone. That music of fiddle and accordion and ceili bands still lifts my spirits and inspires me to follow the Lord of the Dance.

Mother led us in recitation of the Rosary and 'trimmings' each night around an open turf fire. I observed my father on his knees in prayer for a few minutes in the early morning before heading off to his farm work. Missions, processions and novenas provided some excitement before the electric light came and the showbands took over. The phrases 'Thank God', 'Please God', 'With the help of God', 'God save all here', 'God bless the work', punctuated our daily conversations. We were disciplined, corrected and guided in good directions. There was some mild corporal punishment in line with the dominant Catholic ethos of strict discipline. While stealing apples was a seasonal escapade, we were encouraged to be honest and to admit wrongdoing once challenged. Failure to do so meant real trouble. During my life, I have come to appreciate this lesson. Failure by institutions or individuals to own up, confess and repent is at the root of so much evil in relationships, families, churches and society.

Our parents also encouraged us to value reading and education. I was lucky to have an excellent primary school teacher in Cappagh National School from 1949 to 1957. Her name was Annie Gallagher from near Ballaghaderreen, Co Roscommon. She tutored all thirty-five children in a single classroom. Our teacher ensured that there was a regular supply of library books in our small rural school. She was a woman of deep faith and prayer and painted lovely word pictures for us from the Bible for all the mysteries of the Rosary. She had us delivering the 'Far East' and other missionary magazines to homes in the area. She ensured that we served as altar boys in the local parish church. This dedicated teacher gave me additional tuition after school hours which helped me to win a Sligo County Council scholarship in 1957. This enabled me to obtain secondary school education rather than possible emigration to London. She was mild in her use of corporal punishment. However, there were lots of teachers in the country then who were brutal in battering defenceless children. Parents were somewhat cowed and powerless to stop those teachers operating out of malevolence or with tacit approval from Bible and pulpit that if you spared the rod you spoiled the child. It is little wonder that people who were badly treated in any way by lay persons, nuns or priests may be very switched off today from the God behind that version of Catholicism.

St Nathy's College, Ballaghaderreen

My secondary school years from 1957 to 1963 were spent as a boarder in the minor seminary of St Nathy's College Ballaghaderreen, Co Roscommon. It was indeed a rough upheaval to leave home aged twelve and enter a tough new regime in boarding school. The college had a proud record in football and we enjoyed the jousts with St Jarlath's of Tuam, St Muiredeach's of Ballina and Summerhill of Sligo. The college had a number of handball alleys and I really grew to enjoy the game. The staff were mainly Achonry diocesan priests. The deans trained us in a strict regime of absolute obedience to orders, stern discipline and some corporal punishment. Whilst a small number of the priests were inclined to excessive use of corporal punishment, most of the priests gave generously of themselves to educate us and promoted sports, drama, etc. We had daily Mass, prayer and retreats. Sometimes, we served the private masses of the priests at the small side altars. I concentrated on study and sports. Constant hard work on the farm during the holidays and money in short supply left little room for dancing at the crossroads with the comely maidens.

There was very little in the way of career guidance for us. In our final year, priests, missionaries and bishops came to speak to us weekly about joining them on particular missions. Whilst initially my first career choice was for primary teaching, gradually the thought of going forward to priesthood came strongly to my mind. There was no particular pressure from my parents or family to enter ministry, but their deep faith did influence me eventually in that direction. One of the bishops who spoke to us about priesthood was Thomas Drury of San Angelo in West Texas. He was a Sligo man born in Gurteen. I signed up with him for that diocese and the plan was to enter the All Hallows seminary in September 1963 for a seven-year period of preparation for ordination. He became bishop of Corpus Christi, Texas in 1965 and I transferred with him to that diocese on the Gulf of Mexico in South Texas. About fifteen of us from that Leaving Cert class signed up that summer of 1963 for various Irish seminaries and ten of us entered All Hallows College.

All Hallows College in Drumcondra, Dublin was a step up in the world for me after the spartan existence in secondary school. We had our own rooms and the food was much better. The College was founded in 1842 by Father John Hand in order to train priests for service to the Irish emigrants wherever scattered in English-speaking countries. It was staffed and run by the Vincentian Order of priests whose ethos centred on service to the poor and leadership in the ongoing struggle for justice for all. A class of approximately fifty of us from all over Ireland entered that year. An entry exam on the first day determined our ranking for rooms, position in church and refectory for the duration in All Hallows. The authorities picked six of us to attend University College Dublin (UCD) to obtain degrees which might enhance our priestly service as teachers or chaplains. Most seminarians completed Arts degrees to include philosophy, logic and languages. A small number of us opted to proceed with a science degree and I obtained that in 1966. We were indeed a strange cohort of young men then in UCD set apart with our black hats and black outfits. We also completed some philosophy and spirituality studies in the seminary during those years. The education discipline of science with emphasis on experiment, reason and open exploration may have influenced my later development and thinking.

We entered the seminary in the swinging sixties, almost one year after the opening of the historic Second Vatican Council by Pope John XXIII on 11 October 1962. The old seminary education system and Latin language lectures were still in place when we entered. We were still however in a very controlled environment with little access to media. Rules were strict especially regarding avoidance of special friendships or potential homosexual relationships. Recreational walks were always in groups of three or more. It was indeed a long way from the new Ireland with marriage equality. We were concentrating on studies and religious development and probably missed most of the general media stories and excitement of the time.

Gradually, however, change began to happen in liturgical celebration and our seminary training. Staff who themselves had been trained in the old school had to struggle to comprehend and implement the exciting new developments emerging from the Council in Rome. I was deeply influenced by the warm pastoral presence of Pope John XXIII and the hopes aroused by the Council. I liked the idea of "opening up the windows" and updating as an ongoing strategy in the Catholic Church.

The Second Vatican Council (1962-1965) was a seminal event in my faith journey. Many Catholics today were not born then and may have no idea of what we elders are talking about when we speak of Vatican II and its historic importance for modern Catholicism. I suspect that many Catholics of my generation got little information or education as to its meaning from parishes or bishops other than some items they may have picked up from the mass media. In fact, Vatican II was dismissed by some clerics opposed to any reform as providing no change or development from the Penny Catechism. That, however, was a blatant lie and a cruel disservice to Catholic people. Catholic people did indeed experience significant change in the celebration of Mass and other Sacraments. However, the serious developments in doctrine do not appear to have been fully communicated to all Catholics.

2

VATICAN II – CONTEXT AND KEY POINTS

There have been twenty-one General Councils of the Catholic Church with a rich history in terms of changing times and development of doctrine. The first eight beginning with Nicea in 325 were regarded as Ecumenical involving the Catholic Church, East and West, prior to the first major split in the Christian Church in 1054 between Rome and the Orthodox Churches centred on Constantinople. The next thirteen beginning with Lateran I in 1123 are regarded as General Councils. Vatican II is described as Ecumenical since it involved bishops from all over the world and observers from other churches together with lay and religious auditors. The previous Council was Vatican I from Dec 1869 to July 1870. It took place at a time of turmoil in Italy, loss of the Papal States and confinement of the Pope to the Vatican. Pope Pius IX was a reactionary and did not approve of human rights. He was opposed to the Enlightenment and declared war on modernity. Accordingly, Vatican I with 700 bishops in attendance, placed enormous emphasis on the primacy and infallibility of the Pope. The two papal dogmas regarding primacy of papal jurisdiction and infallibility were rushed through on 18 July 1870 despite resistance by many bishops. This led to clericalism and legalism over the following century in the Roman Catholic Church with central control concentrated in the Papacy.

Pope John XXIII was elected in 1958. His warm pastoral presence and emphasis on mercy rather than condemnation brought joy and hope to people in the aftermath of World War II. He realised that the Catholic religion had to be presented in language and concepts intelligible to people in a much-changed world. He stated that there was a constant need for *aggiornamento* or updating. The riches of the early Church needed to be restored from underneath medieval debris and a new narrative of the Christian message needed to be offered to people taking into account the signs of the times. So, he threw open the windows and called the Second Vatican Council very much against the wishes of conservative colleagues and prophets of doom. There were a total of 2,908 eligible Council Fathers in 1962. A total of approximately 2,600 cardinals, archbishops and bishops responded to his call for the opening on 11 October 1962. Italy, with 430 bishops, had the largest delegation. Vatican II was a huge event with an international flavour. Pope John had worldwide popularity and mass media played a huge role to disseminate news and developments from the Council. It was the largest gathering of bishops in the history of the Church and the first without interference from any temporal power.

Curial secretariats were set up to prepare draft documents on relevant topics. Conservative insiders rehashed traditional statements of doctrine and presented them to the assembled bishops. It transpired that the vast majority of the bishops were in the mood for change. They rejected early drafts and broadened out the secretariats in order to produce more up-to-date proposals. The Belgian cardinal, Leo Jozef Suenens, was prominent among the progressive bishops and was an effective promoter of change. He had a keen understanding of the modern world and was able to express it in clear language. At an early session discussing the concept of 'Church', Suenens highlighted the fact that the female half was not represented. Pope John XXIII trusted the judgement of Leo Suenens and his ability to read the signs of the times. There was vigorous debate and much re-writing; parts of the final texts are ambiguous in an effort to accommodate opposing viewpoints.

The four most important documents were called 'Constitutions', namely: *Sacred Liturgy, Church, Divine Revelation* and *Church in the Modern World*. There were nine Decrees and three Declarations. The declarations *Religious Freedom* and *Relationship of the Church to non-Christians* were the most controversial. They represented a major change and development on earlier papal teaching.

Majority voting on fifteen of the sixteen documents was in excess of 2,000 with ten of those at the 2,300 number. Minority voting on ten of the documents was between 2 and 11 bishops. Two documents produced 35 and 39 as opposition and three others stood at 70,75 and 88 as dissenting voices. Accordingly, the documents were all approved by huge voting majorities in favour of reform. The largest minority vote was 164 over against a majority of 1,960 for the *Decree on Instruments of Social Communication* e.g. the press, cinema, radio and television. The mass media were viewed in a very negative fashion in ecclesiastical circles and predominantly from the standpoint of morality. Unfortunately, the minority bishop voters were Vatican insiders and proved very influential in diluting majority wishes and in retaining central Roman control in the following decades.

The *Constitution on the Church* was a crucial foundational document. It started off with the concept that the Church is a mystery, "a reality imbued with the hidden presence of God." It then went on to one of the key changes or advances of the Council, namely, that the Church is the whole People of God. In earlier times, the understanding given to most Catholics was that the Church institution was shaped as a pyramid. The Pope was at the top. The next levels were comprised of cardinals, bishops, priests and religious. The laity were somewhere at ground level. It was great to hear the new emphasis on the dignity of all the baptised and their equal calling to active participation in the mission of Jesus Christ. The old pyramid or clerical model of Church was being replaced with the more inclusive and circular model in tune with the New Testament.

Another very important development within the *Constitution on the Church* related to the role of bishops. Since the time of Vatican

I in 1870, the exercise of Church authority centred on the absolute primacy and infallibility of the Pope allied to powerful Curial control from Rome. Looked at from a wide historical perspective, this absolute papal control was at odds with Church practice for much of the first millennium and the very influential role of Church Councils in the Middle Ages. Clearly, a large majority of bishops had reached a consensus that absolute papal domination was a dangerous historical aberration. Their reading of the signs of the times as well as the advances in Biblical studies and new theological understandings led them to assert their rightful collegial role working in close cooperation with the Pope. Accordingly, it is now stated that the bishops by virtue of their ordination are official representatives of Christ in their dioceses as distinct from being mere employees of the Pope or local branch managers for the Roman Curia.

The *Constitution on the Sacred Liturgy* was the first document to be approved on 4 December 1963 by a vote of 2,147 to 4. There had been some new developments in the field of liturgy over the previous sixty years and the document was easily approved. This document was implemented quickly in parishes. It directly impinged on Catholics since it centred on celebration of Mass - the Liturgy of Word and Eucharist was now in the language of the congregation. All were encouraged into active participation with the priest and invited to sing praise to God with the community rather than recitation of private devotions. The dignity of lay people was further affirmed by reception of Holy Communion in their hand. The People of God were encouraged to give thanks to God together as a community and to encounter the Risen Lord in words, songs, bible and sacraments. It was emphasised that all Catholics were baptised into personal involvement in the mission of Christ and that this should influence all aspects of their family, work, social and political life. Their unique and special talents, charisma and insights were to be harnessed in cooperation with the bishop but not as passive underlings in any clerical system.

The *Constitution on the Church in the Modern World* was a very important document addressed to all people. It now defined the Church as part of God's great world, and not some small elite group against the world and holding it in contempt. The People of God have a mission to serve the whole human family. It represented a crucial step forward away from the ongoing Papal campaigns of the long 19th century against Modernism and the negative clerical approach against so much of the real world in which Catholics were incarnate and doing their best to improve. The document says that modern Christians must read the signs of the times and interpret them in the light of the gospel. It is all in stark contrast to the *Syllabus of Errors*. This document had asserted that the Pope cannot and should not be reconciled and come to terms with progress, liberalism and modern civilisation. For much of the 150 years since that *Syllabus of Errors*, Popes railed against progress, democratic structures, western values and modern civilisation. Catholic thinkers who challenged that particular papal hobby horse against modernism and who advocated that we should read the signs of the times were badly treated by Rome. All priests had to take an oath against modernism. Did the popes of those years unwittingly give a wrong lead to the ultra-loyal Catholics who continue to denounce the evil secular, modern world and poison the well for the vast majority of people working together for progress and doing their best to live wholesome, balanced lives in the real world? Tragically, today, we are conscious of the small group of terrorist extremists from the fundamentalist fringes of another religious tradition who rail and lash out in horrific violence against the open freedoms, modern lifestyle and liberal democratic structures in progressive Western societies.

The *Declaration on Religious Freedom* was a very important declaration and represented a significant development of doctrine away from earlier imperial papal teaching, Crusades, Inquisition and State religions. The Council declared that the human person has a right to religious freedom and that this right is based on the very dignity of the human person. No one could be forced in any way to embrace the Catholic faith. Historical developments such as the American and French revolutions, the Enlightenment, World Wars, Holocaust and the establishment of the United Nations, contributed to this powerful declaration. The world did not stand still even though Pope Pius IX denounced the idea of religious freedom in his infamous *Syllabus of Errors* in 1864. The American Jesuit, John Courtney Murray argued in favour of accepting religious freedom as a basic human right in the years before Vatican II. He was denounced as a Modernist and for daring to contradict the Magisterium. However, the Holy Spirit led the bishops to the concept of religious freedom in Vatican II. John Courtney Murray played a big role in the drafting of the final declaration. It is all a fascinating story of historical change and the development of awareness and doctrine.

New tools and methods to help with the interpretation of Scripture had become available early in the 20th century and were approved by Pope Pius XII in 1943. It seemed sensible to move away from literal Bible interpretation towards a nuanced understanding of history and the human role in assembling the Bible from various oral traditions as well as an appreciation of the different forms of literature contained therein. In the previous centuries after the Reformation, Catholic faith centred on assent to various propositions and doctrines as expounded by the bishops in obedience to the Pope. Personal encounter with God via reading of the Bible was not encouraged and was regarded as a Protestant preserve. The *Constitution on Divine Revelation* opened up the riches of God's ongoing revelation to us in Scripture, Tradition and the wise consensus of the People of God arising from their lived experience. Catholics were encouraged to read and pray the Scriptures together with other Christians. The emphasis was on a personal encounter with the Trinity in their daily lives and in the Scriptures.

The *Declaration on the Relationship of the Church to non-Christians* brought an earth-shattering change of direction and emphasis regarding the Church's relations with the Jews. After the horror of the Holocaust and long centuries of anti-Semitism in the official magisterial teaching of the Roman Catholic Church, this declaration brought a blessed and long overdue change. Here is an example of the awful errors which can arise from certain interpretations of the Bible and unchecked papal pronouncements or magisterial edicts. This declaration also provided a radical new statement that truth is present outside the Body of Christ – the Church and is to be respected wherever it is found in other religions doing good.

The *Decree on Ecumenism* was a major move forward for the Church given all the fractious relationships since the Reformation. It sought restoration of ties with other Christians rather than their return to Rome. It admitted that the blame for separation lay on both sides and called for a change of heart and possible Eucharistic sharing. The document encouraged dialogue and called for the Roman Church to reform itself as part of the process of reunion. Article 6 of the decree was quite explicit in this as follows: "Christ summons the Church, as she goes on her pilgrim way, to that continual reformation of which she always has need, in so far as she is a human institution here on Earth."

Sadly, Pope John XXIII died in June 1963 at a very early stage of the Council. He was succeeded by Pope Paul VI who was a very cautious man and of a totally different disposition. Four crucial items were withdrawn by Pope Paul VI from consideration by all the bishops at the Council. He opted to retain those items within his personal attention and decision. Those four items included: birth control, enforced celibacy for priests, reform of the Curia and collegiality for bishops. Those issues are of huge importance and are very much at the heart of the current crisis in the Roman Catholic Church. The papal decision in the 1968 encyclical *Humanae Vitae* to affirm the traditional clerical teaching about artificial contraception and to disregard the *Report of the Papal Birth Control Commission* has proved to be a hugely negative turning point. The decision in the early 1970s to maintain the practice of enforced celibacy for men called to be priests is now bearing negative fruit with a shortage of priests. The Curia and unaccountable clerical elites retain strong central control instead of being servants of the Pope/Bishops/People of God. Vatican II changed theological understandings, but the older, centralised structures, have continued to exist. The new concepts of the People of God and collegiality of the bishops have not yet been implemented in to modern democratic structures and processes.

More than ever, the content of Vatican II needs to be revisited. Many Catholics are convinced that Vatican II was never promulgated with enthusiasm to the People of God. The legalism, clericalism and excessive emphasis on papal authority of the previous century had led to awful stagnation. The majority of bishops left Rome in 1965 but the conservative hardliners remained in control and blocked full implementation. Prior to Vatican II, the Roman Catholic Church regarded itself as an infallible institution and an unchanging society. Yet, in Vatican II, change happened and it was agreed by massive majorities that doctrinal development is always needed. For readers who wish to study Vatican II in more depth, I recommend *What Happened at Vatican II*, by John O'Malley, as one comprehensive guide and commentary.

3

ALL HALLOWS COLLEGE, 1966-1970

All Hallows College Chapel, Drumcondra

I graduated with a Bachelor of Science degree from UCD in 1966 and began four years of theological training within the confines of the All Hallows seminary. Subjects included dogmatic theology, moral theology, liturgy, biblical studies, Canon Law, preaching and elocution. There were Spanish classes every Friday to prepare those of us destined to serve in predominantly Mexican-American dioceses such as Corpus Christi. We trained in prayer, meditation, spiritual development and celebration of the Eucharist. Sport was also an integral part of our training. Handball, table tennis and hurling were among my favourites. There was much good humour and great camaraderie. There was still little access to the outside world except for those mavericks who sometimes sneaked out at night after lights out to drink or date. I was among the more docile, obedient types and was appointed to the role of assistant sacristan during my first theology year. This was usually taken as a sign that authorities felt you would complete to ordination and fulfil the sacristan role. Summers of 1967 and 1968 were spent in London earning some money to help defray our seminary expenses. My brother Michael obtained jobs for a number of us seminarians in a warehouse and we were also welcomed by uncle Mike, aunt Lucy and cousins. They took us on tours of the city and we explored Hyde Park on a Sunday with all the different orators and evangelists. We enjoyed the late 1960s in swinging London and it was an eye-opening experience. It was a pleasant change and very different world from saving hay and turf on the Ox Mountains or studying dogmatic theology in All Hallows.

Gradually, the changes from Vatican II began to emerge in our training and liturgy celebrations. The Latin textbooks were abandoned and we pursued studies in English. Our Senior Dean and liturgy professor was James Murphy. He favoured text books in liturgy by the English theologian Charles Davis. Fr Davis seemed to have a fine grasp of liturgical developments in the 20th century and a facility to explain those in plain language. We all got a massive shock in 1967 when Charles Davis left the priesthood, married an Anglican woman and produced a challenging book called *A Question of Conscience*. This book raised very troubling questions for us regarding problems within the institution of the Roman Catholic Church. Charles Davis had acquired knowledge regarding the deep Vatican world and it led him out of priesthood and out of the Catholic Church. He was aware of the intrigue and manipulation of Paul VI regarding the *Report of the Birth Control Commission*. A small minority group of traditionalists convinced Paul VI to disregard the report and the final outcome in the 1968 encyclical according to Charles Davis "illustrated the subordination of truth to the prestige of authority and the sacrifice of persons to the preservation of an out-of-date institution." Despite this shock, we continued on our way.

Admittedly, we were gradually losing numbers as some men decided that priesthood was not for them. I remained full of faith and idealism. The model of priesthood as presented by Lacordaire – a French priest – was among those taught to us. The Lacordaire definition of a priest is as follows:

> ...to live in the midst of the world without wishing its pleasures. To be a member of each family yet belonging to none. To share all suffering, to penetrate all secrets. To heal all wounds, to go from men to God and offer Him their prayers. To return from God to men to bring pardon and hope. To have a heart of fire for charity and a heart of bronze for chastity. To teach and to pardon, console and bless always. My God, what a life and it is yours. Priest of Jesus Christ!

It is indeed very idealistic - some would say piety gone mad. Following ordination, I became aware of the faults with that model. It left lay people dependent on the priests and taught them to be passive and docile in the hands of spiritual experts.

The two Vatican II documents regarding priests and priestly formation were very much part of our formation as well. We were deeply conscious of the thousands of priests who had gone before us from All Hallows providing ministry and service. In mid-June each year, many of them returned to All Hallows for Ordination Sunday. It was an opportunity to relive memories and to renew friendships with colleagues. However, the riches and realities of their pastoral experience was not available to us in a structured way. The seminary was very much a holy hothouse and a sheltered bubble with lots of faith and naive idealism. Reality only dawns once you leave the seminary post-ordination and proceed to live in your diocese.

Official Catholic teaching on contraception concerned me as a student and later as a priest. Various forms of contraception have been used for centuries but were always condemned by the Christian Churches. The Catholic hierarchy doubled down on traditional

Catholic opposition to all forms of contraception and Pius XI issued the encyclical *Casti Connubii* in 1930. Without ambiguity, the encyclical tied sexual intercourse to generation of life as the primary aim. In that same year, the Church of England became the first Christian denomination to withhold condemnation of contraception. The Catholic hierarchy took this news as further evidence of Protestant apostasy and total error. Around that time, researchers confirmed the existence of the safe period. This gave rise to use of the rhythm method or periodic continence. Conservative clerics looked askance at this development and were opposed. However, pressure mounted and in 1950 Pius XII speaking to the Italian Catholic Society of Midwives gave explicit approval to the rhythm method. Around 1952, an early form of the birth control pill was produced in America; better forms of the pill were quickly developed. Married people concluded quickly that the rhythm method was unsatisfactory and led to many rhythm babies. By the 1960s, the pill was widely used by couples in America and there was much discussion by lay people. In the early 1960s there were serious calls for the Catholic hierarchy to reconsider its restrictive approach to the pill.

In 1963, William Bekkers, a Catholic bishop in Holland, broke ranks. He said the clerics alone do not have the answers on these complicated issues and that couples should rely on their common sense. Shortly thereafter, the Dutch bishops agreed with Bekkers and stated that the clerics have no immediately appropriate answers to meet all situations and new scientific advances. In the midst of serious debate and questions, Pope John XXIII in March 1963 appointed a six-member Pontifical Commission for the Study of Population, Family and Births, ostensibly to study world population problems and family limitation. Concern for marriage and the family and related matters was definitely on the agenda of the Council but the troubling question of artificial contraception was never opened up for general discussion. Pope John XXIII died in June 1963. Pope

Paul VI removed this item from the agenda of the Council and reserved it for decision by himself after the Pontifical Commission issued a final report. Pope Paul VI expanded the Commission from fifteen in 1964 to seventy-two in 1966. Its composition was mainly priests, but there were thirty-four lay persons including women and married couples. News about the expanding commission and debate about the possibility of doctrinal change circulated increasingly in the media despite Pope Paul VI's assertion that the matter of artificial contraception was only under reflection and that there should be no doubt that the traditional teaching was in place for all eternity. The bishops meeting at Vatican II were removed from the debate and utterly sidelined. The *Constitution on the Church in the Modern World* in 1965 included a holding statement in line with traditional doctrine. Increasingly, the issue and the possibility of change was in the air in the mid-1960s onwards. We were very much aware of it as students of moral theology from 1966 to 1970. After the final session of the Pontifical Commission in June 1966, it issued an official report to Pope Paul VI. While there are not definite figures, the vote appears to have been approximately 64 for versus 4 against of those present at that final meeting. The report recommended a change in the traditional clerical teaching. They had become convinced that artificial contraception should be accepted. Robert McClory, in his book *Turning Point*, summed it up well as follows: "The experts, the married couples, the bishops and cardinals – all appointed by the Pope had spoken with a nearly unanimous voice." An English version of the report was published in the American independent Catholic newspaper *National Catholic Reporter* on 19 April 1967. I found myself very much in agreement with the report and presumed that change was about to happen. That was a foolish and naïve presumption. The Vatican is a different medieval world. A small minority group of powerful insiders and ultra-conservative clerics prepared their own document for Paul VI and rehearsed their arguments against all contraception. However, their key argument was not centred on the morality of contraception. Their chief concern was the appalling vista of an infallible Pope having to acknowledge change or development of doctrine. Paul VI considered all submissions for two years and the speculation about change intensified.

25 JULY 1968 HUMANAE VITAE – BIRTH CONTROL ENCYCLICAL
Driving home from work along Seven Sisters Road, I caught sight of the news headlines that Paul VI had asserted traditional Catholic teaching and condemned all forms of artificial contraception. I was shocked and surprised that the Report had been utterly dismissed. There was shock all over the Catholic world. The issue affected couples in a deeply personal and intimate way at the heart of their marriage and family. The emerging good sense of many Catholic couples as the real experts on love, marriage and family was that the use of contraception was a right option and good moral choice. It slowly began to dawn on people that it was outrageous to allow clerics to intrude in to their bedrooms. People in the developed world were no longer living in fear and began to reject the yoke of clericalism. It was incongruous that a small group of male cardinals in Rome could lay this burden on the shoulders of decent people struggling with all the difficulties of a fast-changing world. People of deep faith in God and steeped in love became very disheartened. The debate and dissent began to grow and continues to this day. It turned out to be a historic turning point and caused many married Catholics to question the relevance of Church teaching to their married lives. The papal teaching on artificial contraception has not been accepted or assented to within the consensus of the faithful.

The encyclical became a hot topic of debate. I was deeply troubled by this turn of events in an opposite direction to the changes, developments and hopes we all experienced with Vatican II.

I had completed some Legion of Mary visitation of homes and families during my summers working in London. I could see the rough, crowded conditions of some families and the absolute need for a safe method of responsible family limitation. I remained deeply disturbed by *Humanae Vitae* and its aftermath. Before returning to the seminary in early September 1968, I wrote a letter to *The Irish Press* expressing my doubts and concerns and discussed the letter with my parents. To my surprise, they both agreed with me. They had followed the debate in the public media and had come to the conclusion that couples should be able to use modern methods of artificial contraception. They remained a devout Catholic couple but were prepared to disagree privately with purely clerical teaching on a non-core issue. They felt far more qualified than any cleric to reach a responsible moral decision on this very important family issue. The letter was published on Saturday 21 September 1968 and the text is as follows:

THE POPE'S DECISION

Letters to The Editor
The Irish Press, Saturday, 21 September 1968

I have just read Mr. O'Dalaigh's interesting letter (September 2). He says, "The Holy Father is right! I make this statement as the father of a large family and as an Irishman who believes in Irish traditional Catholicism." While I ponder the logic of this statement, Bob Dylan proclaims over the radio, "The times, they are a-changin'...". And I start a-thinkin'.

Yes, indeed! The world is changing and so is Ireland and the Irish people, thank God. Consequently, the Catholic Church in Ireland must change and develop. This change and development is something to be welcomed, because whenever there is evolution and change there is life. The reality to be feared is stagnation. It signifies death. People are more educated today and the world is growing away from the superstitions, fears and taboos of past ages. People today are using their God-given faculties of reason and intelligence.

Accordingly, in Czechoslovakia, a brave people who desire to remain socialists, stand up and ask why this cannot be combined with freedom of expression, etc. Similarly, within the Catholic Church, people who are and intend to remain committed Christians, look at the problems of the real world in which they live, ask awkward questions and seek honest, mature discussion. These cannot be silenced by wielding the heavy hand of authority. That age is past, thank God. Few would believe that these people are "imperialist agents" either. These Christians believe that Our Lord did give "authority" to his apostles and their successors, but they also believe that it was intended as a radically different type of authority to that of secular rulers. Those Christians are also honest and sincere.

We all know that genuine honesty and sincerity can cut deep and hurt. Similarly, genuine honesty and sincerity can often cut across the deeply entrenched positions and traditions of a particular institution. This openness to truth is perhaps a very necessary form of self-denial today.

Following on this, I'd imagine it is easy for any priest or bishop to accept and promulgate the Pope's guidelines. After all, it doesn't affect priests or bishops. For laymen and priests alike, it is easier to stick by the establishment and to uphold the prestige of the good old institution, by at least giving external assent. But some Christians look further afield, and venture into the more uncomfortable world outside the Holy Roman Empire. Those Christians "know where the Lord's table is, but they do not know where the Lord is not". So they meet families whose homes are hovels. They encounter families who exist in single rooms, in overcrowded streets of London, and the other glamour cities of the world. These Christians realise, Mr. O'Dalaigh, that such living *conditions are a far cry from the comfort and social standing of a named house in suburban Athlone. They meet families in the shacks of Bogota. They hesitate before preaching your lovely theory of married love and restraint to a man and woman whose only comfort is themselves in the darkness and squalor of a crowded hut on the outskirts of Lima. These Christians do not term themselves intellectuals, Mr. O'Dalaigh. They are Christians with eyes open to the woeful problems of men and women today. They also have a healthy, modern, Christian attitude towards sex. They study "Humanae Vitae", compare it with the harsh, real world and are puzzled. They seek understanding and compassionate answers for the many problems still unresolved. I know a young Catholic couple deeply in love with one another. They have one badly deformed child. Doctors have told them that another child will be in a similar condition. What are these two people to do for the rest of their married lives? Buy single beds and specially-bound copies of "Humanae Vitae"? "Humanae Vitae" is supposed to be a document filled with compassion and understanding for the problems of married people. This couple have failed to discover this compassion. But of course, they are only a married couple, and do not have the wonderful insights of the experts on marriage! So Mr. O'Dalaigh, we must pray for those people who will inevitably pander to their evil, animal, lower nature, and express their love and support for one another through sexual intercourse!*

So with problems such as this in mind, I ponder the Pope's weighty decision and ask questions. I know that this is not in best Irish Catholic traditional methods, but I fail to see anything un-Christian in this reflection and questioning.

JOSEPH MULVANEY
Cabra,
Coolaney,
Co. Sligo.

As you may suspect, the letter did indeed land me in lots of hot water. My bishop was informed in Corpus Christi about the letter and he instructed All Hallows authorities to deal with me. The Senior Dean interrogated and scolded me and mocked my impertinence as a young seminarian. I expressed my concerns about married couples in difficult circumstances. That did not seem to matter much over against a clerical magisterium with infallible authority. I still felt called to ministry and priesthood. I was forced to concede that perhaps it was not wise or right to question papal teaching. The Vincentian authorities were not big into Inquisition and only issued a yellow card. They voted to allow me to continue my studies towards the priesthood.

Our academic, spiritual and pastoral training continued apace en route to Subdeaconate/Deaconate in 1969 and Priestly Ordination in 1970. The staff were all holy men and qualified academics in their field. However, few of them had much pastoral experience. They lived as Vincentians in community and were not in a position to talk to us about the lonely realities of celibate life in far-flung isolated outposts after ordination. Our training concerning celibacy was minimal apart from a Latin stricture about not being alone with a woman and never congregating in twos as seminarians. Holy priests gave us wonderful idealistic talks and spiritual motivation, but there were no lectures or workshops by experienced pastoral priests concerning the realities of priestly life. The seminary authorities were operating out of a medieval meaning system and were not equipped to prepare us properly for celibate life as a priest in foreign countries and a fast-changing world. Absolute self-sacrifice for the cause and spiritual sublimation of normal sex instinct allied to lots of hard work, prayer, golf and clerical camaraderie was supposed to enable us to cope with a lifetime without wife or intimacy. Most of us, as far as I am aware, followed the maxim of our spiritual directors during our seminary years that we should not go dancing or date any woman if we were

39

serious about giving our vocation a chance. I know I followed that advice. I did not date or go dancing to the showbands and exciting summer carnivals. However, this obedient observance may well have hampered the normal pathways to growth, sexual development and emotional maturity for some of us seminarians. However, we were all full of faith, sincere and idealistic. We wanted to help people encounter the Risen Christ in the Eucharist, sacraments and parish community. We wanted to celebrate, give thanks and do good for people. We proceeded on our way, trusting in the Lord. The All Hallows blessing rang in our ears – "May you die wondering."

During our final two years of theology from 1968 to 1970, we were introduced to some pastoral work in the general area surrounding Drumcondra. We joined the Legion of Mary, Society of St. Vincent de Paul and youth groups operating with lay volunteers in their pastoral work. I was assigned to work for a few hours each Sunday with one of the patients in Grangegorman Mental Hospital. Some Sundays, we delivered homilies as trainee deacons in High Park, an adjacent convent institution. We knew virtually nothing about the persons within the institution and saw only pale female faces in the darkened church from our vantage point in the pulpit. High Park was what was to become known as a Magdalene Laundry. The Magdalene Laundries in Ireland, also known as Magdalene asylums, were institutions of confinement usually run by Catholic orders of nuns which operated from the 18th to the late 20th centuries. They were run ostensibly to house 'fallen women', an estimated thirty thousand of whom were confined in those institutions in Ireland. In 1993, a mass grave containing 155 corpses was uncovered in the High Park convent grounds. This led to media revelations about the operations of the secretive institutions. A formal state apology was issued in 2013. There remain many unanswered questions about High Park and all the laundries. It appears that terrible wrong was done to those women. We were naïve young men and knew nothing of the Magdalene Laundries regime and the culture of Catholic Ireland behind the laundries. We had been programmed with so much faith and idealism. It was only much later that we all became aware of the darker side of the Catholic Church. This spurs me on now to speak out for open investigation and reform throughout the Catholic Church. The maltreatment of women needs to be confronted once and for all.

During August of 1969, I was fortunate to be assigned to spend a month acquiring pastoral experience as a deacon in a parish in Luton, England. I was privileged to meet and learn from two Irish pastoral priests in that parish – Fr Liam Murtagh from Sligo and the late Fr Tom Colreavy from Leitrim. There were many Irish emigrants in the parish together with many other nationalities. There was excellent parish ministry and we did plenty of parish visitation in the afternoons and evenings. This work is difficult and there are obvious problems doing it today but it is a wonderful way to reach out, serve, listen and get to know the people of a parish.

September 1969 to June 1970 was a busy and exciting time for me as we entered the last lap of preparation for ordination. We looked forward with joy and excitement to the big day for us and our families. Families, friends and past men gathered in the seminary on that beautiful sunny day. Bishop McKeon and past men of the college laid hands on us as part of the ordination mass and we emerged as ordained priests to celebrate in the beautiful, peaceful surroundings of All Hallows. It was indeed an honour, a blessing and a privilege for me to be ordained as an All Hallows priest. I joined a cadre of almost 4,000 priests who had gone forth from 1842 onwards to raise the Banner of the Lord Jesus Christ. After dinner and a final farewell, the scattering of the class of 1970 began and we travelled out to the four corners of Ireland. Bonfires blazed on the road from Collooney to a reception at the local parish church. Sligo had not won the All-Ireland, but it was a special occasion for our family and parish. First

Mass on 15 June 1970 was a parish celebration and wonderful personal experience. A community banquet in Coolaney Technical School rounded off the festivities.

First Mass at Church of the Sacred Heart and St Joseph, Rockfield, Coolaney, County Sligo

4

DIOCESE OF CORPUS CHRISTI, TEXAS, 1970-1974

Corpus Christi Cathedral   Texas State Aquarium and Corpus Christi Waterfront

I travelled to Corpus Christi, Texas in August 1970 together with the late Fr Morgan Rowsome (from Camolin Co. Wexford). It felt like stepping into a steam oven when we emerged into the Texas heat of Corpus Christi airport. It took me years to adapt to the high Texas heat and humidity. We were welcomed by Irish priests serving in the diocese since the mid-1950s and ordained in various Irish seminaries. The diocese was served by about twenty-five Irish priests and a larger cohort of Irish nuns who had served over a long number of years in the areas of education and health. There were also American, Mexican-American and Spanish priests as well as a large contingent of Oblate Fathers in various missions around Texas.

I was assigned to a Mexican-American parish - Our Lady of Guadalupe – which was situated in the westside suburbs of Corpus Christi. There was much poverty and deprivation in our area and Hurricane Celia which hit Corpus Christi one day after my arrival caused much devastation. In the early weeks, I was helping to run a Red Cross centre in the parish and distributing much needed food and supplies. I got down to parish work at once, using the Spanish I had learned in All Hallows and Spain to celebrate Mass, baptisms, weddings, funerals and family events such as First Communion, Confirmation and the *Quinceañera* which is a Hispanic tradition celebrating a young girl's coming of age at fifteen. The people may have got away with murder in confession since my Spanish was not by any means perfect. Teaching and helping with the Christian Doctrine classes for young people attending State Schools was mainly in English.

I discovered a Catholicism much different to our traditional Irish Catholicism and the updated Catholicism we seminarians had absorbed post-Vatican II. I tried to learn as quickly as I could about Mexican-American culture and religion. Mexican-American or Latin Catholicism does not have the same rigid adherence to Sunday Mass or practice. Although they have great faith in *El Señor Jesucristo*, they place much emphasis on devotion to the Virgin Mary, shrines, statues, holy water and candles. Some are deferential to clergy and religious and they surprised me by genuflecting and kissing my hand. Many of the men seldom darkened the door of the church. Religion appeared to be only for the females. However, once a tragedy happened such as an accident or cantina killing the important pastoral practice was to be comforting and welcoming for the bereaved in their crisis time. The rectory doorbell could ring at any hour of the day or night with requests for corporal or spiritual help. It was important to visit the sick and old in their homes or in hospital. They valued the prayer and blessing of the priest. The important pastoral approach was to signal, even with broken Spanish, that you respected people and their language. There was some discrimination against them in the dominant Anglo-Texan culture and much pressure to speak English. Marriage preparation sessions and provision of all certificates were also part of a busy rectory life. We were often invited to homes for family celebrations and it was great to enjoy their food and hospitality.

A colleague of mine, Fr Willie Gough, an alumnus of All Hallows, took me under his wing as I floundered a bit during my first year adapting to a new culture, climate and a world very different from the camaraderie of earlier seminary years. He proved to be a very good friend and mentor. Fr Gough introduced me to Mexican food; I was very wary at first but grew to love it. While his health was poor, he was a warm-hearted pastor. He was well-read in literature and church matters and an excellent preacher. His rectory was a great meeting place for Irish priests. There was much debate and discussion among us about ongoing developments in the church and ministry in an evolving situation post-Vatican II. There were lots of exciting developments in the American Church, with the civil rights struggle and anti-Vietnam war groups all very active and topical. Relationships between priests and their bishops became strained in those turbulent post-Vatican II years and so much speeded up change in the world and society around us. Sadly, Fr Gough's health deteriorated, and he died at a relatively young age in 1982.

Tuesdays were generally our day off. It was very important for health and sanity to get a break on that day. Normally, a dozen or more of us Irish priests gathered at a golf course in the morning. After golf and a *siesta,* we would all meet in the evening for a meal. Later, we'd adjourn to some rectory to play the traditional Irish card game of 25. The late-night camaraderie added to the fun and freed up some honest sharing of the realities of their priestly life and ministry. This Tuesday fellowship provided male bonding and sound pastoral advice together with shared news and sport from Ireland. Clerical gossip and news of spats with the bishop were also in the mix. In the wee small hours, the men dispersed to their busy urban parishes or their lonely outposts way out long miles into the Texas boondocks. Our bishop appeared to be somewhat remote from us priests and principally concerned with administration and high affairs of Church in the Chancery Office. However, I have a good memory of myself and Morgan Rowsome invited to Christmas dinner with him in December 1970. Mother Patricia, an elderly Irish nun, cooked up a delicious turkey. Bishop Drury played the accordion and Morgan and I melted in the Texas heat in the front garden of his abode overlooking the Gulf of Mexico. It was indeed a long way from a deep and dark December in Coolaney, Sligo or Camolin, Co Wexford.

An important part of my priestly work during that first year in Corpus Christi involved officiating at the funerals of Vietnam War soldiers. The Vietnam War was at its height and there was a large number of Mexican-American young men in the military. It was a savage war and the body bags of remains were returning to Corpus Christi and elsewhere with awful frequency. Once or twice a week, we had to attend at the airport and the local funeral home to receive and wake the remains of a parishioner. It was a dreadful time for the community and there was massive grief. The following morning there was the Mass and full military honours later at the burial in the cemetery. This experience of war, waste and the awful grief of families really shook me up as a young priest. The month-long summer 1971 holiday in Ireland couldn't come soon enough but I arrived home to the devastation of war in Northern Ireland.

On return to Corpus Christi in August 1971, the bishop assigned me to help out Father John McHugh as an assistant pastor in Sacred Heart parish, Sinton. It was an Anglo or white Texan parish in a small town about 30 miles from Corpus Christi. Fr John from Co Galway had an excellent reputation over a long number of years as a great pastor and devout man of prayer. He had temporarily lost his voice and I was assigned to be his assistant for a year. My arrival coincided with another hurricane named Fern which caused much flooding and destruction. Once again, my first months were spent assisting the Red Cross with relief and supplies for the affected area.

Fr John continued to receive treatment and his written notes of instruction peppered the silence. John and I celebrated Masses and the good man suffered in silence at my sermons.

In this parish, I was blessed to meet Judy and Farrah ("Vic") Vickers and their family. I was warmly welcomed into their home. They lived on a lovely farmstead in the flat plains a few miles out of Sinton. They introduced me to the best of American and Texan country music including Kris Kristofferson, Waylon Jennings and Willie Nelson. Later, I got to love Mexican country and mariachi music with a special liking for the soft crooning of Freddie Fender. Their hospitality and friendship was invaluable at a time when I was beginning to experience loneliness and doubts in my new priestly existence. Fr John recovered his voice and mojo by early summer 1972 and I was transferred to the Mexican-American parish of St Anthony's in Robstown, Texas.

By that summer of 1972, I was becoming troubled about various aspects of the priestly life. I was beginning to mature and grow up in the real world as a heterosexual man. I was becoming increasingly uncomfortable in my clerical role and being placed on a pedestal as holy witchdoctor or magic man or shaman. I wanted to be in the real world and not a species apart from my brothers and sisters. The official clerical teaching on artificial contraception with which I disagreed in the seminary was now becoming very problematic for me. While many strong Catholic couples were unafraid to make their own decisions in good conscience, I became aware that some devout and vulnerable Catholics were struggling with scrupulous observance of clerical doctrine in very difficult circumstances. I became ashamed of myself as a cowardly collaborator with the Pharisees and religious authorities in the Gospels whom Jesus castigated for laying burdens on innocent shoulders and doing nothing to help. I saw the growing conflict for married people around the hugely important issues of responsible parenthood, sexuality and world population control. I knew that the small minority group in Rome could never concede that the Anglican Church read the signs of the times better in 1930 and had the insight to move forward on this issue. During the summer holiday, I talked with parents and family. They were shocked, disappointed and very alarmed at the change in my outlook and thinking. They advised that I should continue in priesthood for at least another two years and give my best effort. I returned to my parish in August 1972 and resolved to do my best over the following years.

I was lucky to be assigned to work with an Irish pastoral team. The pastor was a fellow Sligo man named Seamus McGowan. The other assistants were Tom Davis and Peter McNamara. Fr Seamus assigned us all to various ministries in the parish. It was indeed a busy place. The work was similar to my first posting in Our Lady of Guadalupe only on a much larger scale. We had six Masses and numerous baptisms on a Sunday. There was a program of parish visitation and home blessings and work in the schools and youth groups. The doorbell of the rectory rang at all hours and the emergency call out was frequent to accidents or hospital. We all helped out even at the bingo fundraising on a Friday night.

There was some growing political controversy in the town as young Mexican-American men began to become more involved politically asserting La Raza pride and I became interested in that cause. An element of racism and discrimination was still in the public realm and there was Anglo political control on City Council and school boards even though there was a majority Mexican-American populace if they used their vote. While I encouraged prayer, I also preached that they should then get up off their knees and find non-violent political ways to counter injustice and improve the lot of Hispanic people. I had read the books of the liberation theologians in South America and felt they had a strong case. I was also very impressed by the document produced by the Synod of Bishops in

1971 entitled *Justice in the World*. A key phrase from that document struck me strongly then and has stayed with me to this day:

Action on behalf of justice and participation in the transformation of the world fully appears to us as a constitutive dimension of the preaching of the Gospel, or, in other words, of the Church's mission for the redemption of the human race and its liberation from every oppressive situation.

That can be our motto as we work to end injustices and oppressive situations in the Catholic Church and in society. My involvement, even on the fringes of politics in Robstown, was not welcomed by some people in the area and Bishop Drury instructed me to desist from any political involvement. All four of us continued with our pastoral work. I enjoyed celebrating the Eucharist in the church as well as home visitation and parish social work. I looked forward to the small informal group Masses in the homes of parishioners. This setting allows for dialogue and discussion and personal communication. The presence of God becomes more real when people freely gather in small family-like groups in the name of Jesus. Counselling and Confession was much in demand. I hoped that I was of some value in those encounters with people. It was a privilege and a blessing to celebrate with people in the happy events as a priest. It was humbling and rewarding as a priest to bring some small measure of consolation and support at times of tragedy and death.

I continued to follow as much as possible the happenings, events and trends in the American Church. The Synod of Bishops in 1971 had issued a document *The Ministerial Priesthood* in which they confirmed that celibacy would continue to be required of any man who felt called to serve as a priest and that priestly ordination of married men is not to be permitted. Huge numbers of priests and nuns around this time were leaving priesthood and religious life. It was a time of change and upheaval. In 1973 the news broke in our diocese that my former pastor in Sinton – Fr John McHugh – was leaving the clerical state and was planning to marry. This news came as a shock to us all; he was going to be a huge loss to priestly ministry in the diocese and all were going to miss him. Clearly, this priest had the charism or gift of ministry and was very happy working as a priest. He now wished to marry and that forced him out of official priesthood and work which he loved. John and Delfina married and settled down to raise a family in Corpus Christi. He was enabled by sympathetic confrères to continue to provide some service in various parishes.

By the summer of 1974, I knew that it was getting close to decision time for me. I was aware that some priests who were unhappy in ministry, had delayed their decision to leave for various reasons. Sadly, some reached a point where it was too late in terms of prospects for a relationship or career change. There are solid reasons to delay even if you have reached the conclusion that priesthood is not for you. All of us want to honour our vows even though such commitments may have arisen from ignorance of post-ordination realities or cultural conditioning or hyped-up faith and naive idealism. No one wants to be called Judas or a failure. A priest may feel trapped with nowhere to go. Most priests have no degrees or professional qualifications to enable them to earn a living in a new career. Priests are poorly paid and there is little in terms of savings. There is no significant severance money if you decide to leave the priesthood. Then, there was serious consideration of potential pain, embarrassment and opprobrium for parents and family back in Ireland. I heard the joke cracked at late night sessions "ah shure, you wouldn't do it to your poor oul mother back in Ireland!" Waiting for her to die is not a good scenario but the group in our Catholic Church who insist on enforced celibacy appear to have little empathy for fellow men in painful human scenarios. They may have lots of compensations within a sheltered Vatican cocoon in terms of power, authority, control, etc. and may care very little about the suffering of other priests. We should all carefully note that the Church defined as the People of God does not demand celibacy of their priests and have not voted for this law.

While I had worked hard for the two years in Robstown and found reward in much of the priestly work, I had reached a conclusion that the celibate life was not one in which I could continue. I think it is cruel and unfair on men who are called by God to serve as priests, but who do not have the stoic ability to live out their lives in service as celibate men. Whilst parish life was extremely busy, at the end of the day I was faced with the stark reality of a solitary existence; a future of being part of a couple was never going to be an option. I experienced loneliness as a growing issue and this was no longer assuaged by clerical camaraderie, golf, hard work and prayer.

Allied to the realities of priestly life, it was becoming increasingly difficult to preach justice when there clearly remains inequality for women in the Catholic Church. I was unable to collaborate in homophobia and the exclusion of divorced and separated persons from the Lord's Supper. I had observed and listened closely to my fellow priests in the diocese. There was no doubt about the wonderful service and pastoral ministry provided by those men. However, I saw some men suffering and twisted and seeking compensation under the unfair burden. I was aware of some of the secrets, struggles and pain. I saw cases of arrested development and heard from classmates in various countries about some of the weird and autocratic pastors they had encountered in their early assignments. Those priests were victims of a cold clerical system opposed for centuries to modern insights, progress and enlightenment. The bishops seem remote, are sworn to the party line and give priority to administration. I feel very strongly that the bishops should give top priority to genuine care for their priests in the broadest possible sense. The priests will then, most likely, take good care of the people.

As stated earlier, my family were aware of my changed outlook. In those early 1970s, they listened to many debates and discussions on radio and the Late Late Show. The weekly Late Late Show hosted by Gay Byrne on Irish national television from 1962 onwards, provided a forum for open discussion on serious and controversial issues. Church and State officials did not like the questions or the spotlight. However, the people hungry for truth and honesty loved the programmes. The Late Late provided a secular forum for discussion of religious issues when secrecy, censorship and silence was the prevailing Catholic ethos. The people of Ireland learned of the huge exodus of priests and religious. I think this information was of much benefit to my parents, family and home parish. It helped them to understand some of the context and wider world within which I was experiencing some difficulty. Gay Byrne and the Late Late Show did the State and Church a great service.

Thankfully, despite their personal worries and disappointment, my parents were able to state to me by letter in August 1974 that they only wanted for me to be healthy and happy and doing good down whatever road I chose to travel. I applied to Bishop Drury for a leave of absence or sabbatical in August 1974 which was subsequently granted. I bid farewell to my confrères and the good people of St Anthony's in September 1974 around the same time Richard Nixon waved farewell to the White House post-Watergate.

5

CITY OF CORPUS CHRISTI, 1974-1977

I commenced the leave of absence from clerical duties in September 1974. This provided time and space to work in a different field and gain further experience. It gave me an opportunity to reconsider everything and to see if I wished to return to working as a priest, which still remained open to me as an option. My good friends Judy and Vic Vickers provided me with immediate accommodation, advice and support. The bishop had directed that I should move out of the Corpus Christi area while on the leave of absence. However, Judy and Vic and other friends advised that I should remain in Corpus Christi where I had settled and had a support base of priest and lay friends. I found an apartment in Corpus Christi and, eventually, by December 1974 acquired employment as an Administrative Assistant/ Counsellor with the City of Corpus Christi. Catholic contacts helped me towards this job and it was a blessing to work with a team led by a prominent Catholic lay woman named Mary Whitmire. The new job entailed working with disadvantaged persons from the general Corpus Christi region. Some of them were from parishes in which I had served. The idea was to place them for training and work experience for approximately six months in public sector positions. The program was federally funded under the Comprehensive Employment & Training Act. Our task was to help eligible disadvantaged persons through training, counselling and work experience to find full-time employment elsewhere in the private or public sector but off our program payroll at the end of six months. I very much enjoyed the challenge of working with employers and disadvantaged persons. I began to expand my social life and it was great to proceed with a normal life and develop new relationships.

I had plenty of time to read Catholic newspapers and periodicals as to the emerging stories post-Vatican II. Many priests and nuns had become involved with the civil rights struggle in the United States in the 1960s and were inspired to work for social justice based on the gospels and Church social justice documents. Priests and nuns were very aware of the all-pervasive problems of racism as well as the deepening crisis over war, Vietnam and gun violence. Action for social justice in civil society inevitably brought the spotlight on the Roman Catholic institution and many injustices therein especially towards women. All reports seemed to indicate that religious sisters in the United States had taken Vatican II very seriously. They had studied the documents and later commentaries in detail. They seemed to move in a very open and collegial manner in their congregations to implement change. Those were all strong women of faith, prayer and love. They had provided great service to the poor for over a century. A small number remained wedded to the past and had been hurt under a cold and abnormal regime. Most were feminists way ahead of their time and knew that there is a serious problem within the patriarchal systems and structures of the Catholic Church. Meanwhile, the male clerics seemed to move at a much slower pace towards acceptance, understanding and implementation of Vatican II. It is true that they were busy with priestly work and signals from higher-up clerics appeared to be putting brakes on change and reform. Priests are sworn to obedience within the clerical club and do not have the independence of female religious communities. Many of the priests had been trained in the old school and probably had little opportunity to consider Vatican II in serious detail. I still maintained contact with classmates scattered worldwide. I met regularly with my priest friends and listened to their point of view. Like the vast majority of priests today, they continued to provide great pastoral ministry, but they knew in their hearts that change was needed. It was most interesting to listen to their honest thinking about various religious issues and the weird coldness of a dysfunctional club. Priests as clerics are not free to voice their honest thinking on those and other issues in public.

In the book *Eunuchs for the Kingdom of Heaven: The Catholic Church and Sexuality*, Uta Ranke-Heinemann, a German theologian, elaborates on the evolution of celibacy. Catholic celibacy has pagan roots. There were traditions to do with ritual purity and marital intercourse was regarded as impure. Over the course of the first millennium, there arose an attitude of hostility to sex and marriage on the part of leading theologians and popes. The monastic tradition had developed where communities dedicated themselves to particular services. Totally negative attitudes towards sex and women by various Popes led eventually to the introduction of enforced celibacy in 1139. This was a purely man-made law and copper-fastened by the Council of Trent in 1545. It met with much resistance and all kinds of stratagems to get around an unjust law over the following centuries. Today in the developed world of human rights, expanded employment opportunities and open media, people are more aware of the injustice of the law and the wrong behaviour which may result. Such people are in favour of immediate change of a man-made rule. There is no doubt that such change could be introduced by the People of God.

Based on various sociological reports on priesthood and my own observations, I would construct the following profile in regard to priests:

1. Some men are called and gifted to both priesthood and celibacy. They give totally of themselves to the Lord and to the people. We are all blessed by their pastoral ministry.

2. Many men are called to priesthood and marriage. Discovery of this reality years after ordination means priests feel trapped with no options in terms of career or relationship. They want to honour their commitment at ordination. Some

make the most of it and stoically carry on with priesthood. It is obviously dangerous as a priest to blow the whistle or to rock the boat. You will be punished and ostracised; the pressure is powerful to maintain the status quo with loyal adherence to the party line. There is a measure of safety and security and, maybe, even, some compensations. Publicly, the façade remains in place and lay people or bishops may never know the truth. However, their unhappiness in an unjust situation may negatively impact their mental health and efficacy as a priest. Tragically, some of those men have committed suicide.

3. The abnormal and all-male seminary training with a strong component of suspicion and hostility towards women is a dangerous tampering with normal sexuality. The result can be a small number of predator or paedophile priests at an arrested stage of sexual development and hooked on control.

4. Some heterosexual priests may find a kind of half-way house or "arrangement" where they carry on with priesthood but somehow manage to have a relationship or companionship with a woman below the radar or sometimes even hiding in plain sight. This option is difficult to maintain but has been achieved. Then you look further afield to countries and cultures where the Catholic rule for priests is regarded as utterly abnormal and unnatural. Anecdotally, as priests we would have heard stories from countries in Africa, Latin America and others where the priest continued to work but also has a wife or companion and children. It is acceptable to the good sense of the people but the "wink and nod" ethos must go on in the face of Roman intransigence.

5. Studies and reports appear to indicate that an unusually large and disproportionate percentage of priests are homosexual. No question is raised by people or bishop if such priests

socialise, recreate, work and live together in rectories. However, major questions and holy hassle arise if a heterosexual priest socialises, works, recreates, travels in car or lives in a rectory alone with a woman. This is the end of the world – the woman is major trouble ever since the Garden of Eden.

I have outlined in the previous chapter elements of my discomfort and unease as a cleric. I retained my faith in Jesus Christ and liked to work as a priest bringing God's presence, love, mercy, peace and consolation to people. However, I was increasingly uncomfortable in my role as a cleric and as a member of a separate clerical caste. I was uncomfortable with clerical control and claims by any human group or institution to pre-eminence and infallibility. I favoured more active involvement and decision-making for all baptised Christians. I was very uncomfortable with some of the Bible readings. It seemed so out of sync and antiquated to impose some Old Testament texts on people trying to survive and looking for meaning in a tough modern world. There could be as many interpretations as there are priests and preachers. Practically any daft thesis can be "proved" by anybody who takes single one-liners from the Bible in a literal fashion. Some texts and personal interpretations appear to verge dangerously close to nonsense especially when there is no right to respond.

However, a crucial issue emerging for me centred on loneliness. I had been blessed to be born out of a good marriage and into a loving family. I was attracted to women and wanted the intimate companionships of marriage. My own personal experience and my observation of fellow priests led me to the conclusion that enforced or mandatory celibacy is an injustice to men called to priesthood. I concluded that it is dangerous to tamper with or suppress normal, healthy sexuality by forcing a man to live a celibate life. There is a real danger that compensation such as power, authority and control may be expected by the cleric. The problem is *enforced* or *mandatory* celibacy. There is no problem with freely-chosen celibacy so long as it is not based on negative teaching about sexuality or women or the premise that virginity is the superior way. It is wonderful if a person freely chooses to remain celibate in the service of people for a limited number of years or for a lifetime. Many people today volunteer years of their life in loving service to people. That is appropriate once it is a free choice by a mature adult with full and complete knowledge. However, the problem in the Catholic Church is that the Pope and Roman Curia have made a package deal of priesthood and celibacy and arrogantly expect God to bestow the package deal on the candidate for priesthood. The charisms or gifts of priesthood and celibacy are two separate and distinct talents as admitted in the Vatican II *Decree on the Ministry and Life of Priests*. In chapter III, paragraph 16, referring to perpetual continence it states:

> *It is not, indeed, demanded by the very nature of the priesthood, as is evident from the practice of the primitive Church and from the tradition of the Eastern Churches. In Churches, in addition to bishops and those others who by a gift of grace choose to observe celibacy, there also exist married priests of outstanding merit.*

We were very aware of that statement by the bishops, and the super pious sentiments which followed it maintaining the clerical discipline. In the light of the above statement of fact, it remains supremely arrogant and foolish for the Roman Curia to continue to try to force God's hand and insist that God must bestow both charisms on the man who feels called to priesthood. The disciples and apostles around Jesus were free to marry. Many Catholics are aware of the outdated and negative reasoning behind this law from 1139 onwards. Many Catholic people are realistic enough to know that this law is also about institutional property rights and cheap obedient labour to be moved around at will in service to a multi-national institution and easy control of good-hearted men deliberately deprived of wise women or strong partners to provide strength and support. Good priests are not free to speak their truth about the negative realities. However, following their conscience, the silence and severe reluctance over the past decades of most priests to joyfully encourage fellow men into the priesthood as currently structured speaks volumes for those with ears to hear. Accordingly, over the past decades Catholic parents are very reluctant to encourage their sons into an unbalanced, dysfunctional system. Catholic families know it is time to abandon the injustice of enforced celibacy. Catholic families can pray that the Holy Spirit will guide the bishops to accompany us on our pilgrim way and acknowledge that it is indeed way past time to change on this issue and other clerical traditions or teachings as well. I know some clerics and their ultra-loyal supporters will still argue that celibacy is freely-chosen by men today going for ordination. That is a lie and a con trick; it is not genuinely freely chosen until you see Roman Catholic (not former Anglican) married and celibate priests functioning together in the Catholic Church. It should be left truly optional.

The leave of absence and my work with the city of Corpus Christi proved a worthwhile experience for me. It was an opportunity for me to grow and develop new friendships. By March 1976, I had reached the decision that I wanted to leave the priesthood. Accordingly, I wrote to bishop Drury stating my decision and requesting due process of dispensation. I met with him and his Chancellor Monsignor William Thompson. Both men indicated to me that I would have difficulty getting the dispensation if I remained living and working in Corpus Christi. Those two priests were implementing official Roman policy at that time to make it very difficult in terms of employment and support for any priest who decided to leave the ministry. The cruel policy was to make you leave the area in which you had worked as a priest. I valued and enjoyed my work as an employee of the City of Corpus Christi.

I prepared a lengthy letter for the Vatican authorities giving my honest reasons as detailed earlier for leaving the clerical state and requiring a dispensation. In October 1976, I received a letter from the Chancellor stating that my request had not been immediately granted and that Rome was in the process of interviewing my professors in the seminary in Ireland, in pursuit of further information. Monsignor Thompson stated that he suspected the delay and refusal was motivated by my critical attitude about certain Roman teachings and structures. I should have known that it is potentially dangerous to utter any honest criticism of the official Curia line on any issue.

However, a blessing had come into my life in the form of a beautiful woman. I first met Maureen Leonard at a St Patrick's Day gathering in 1975 for Irish people in the Corpus Christi area. She was the principal of a local Catholic School. Maureen hailed from Killasolan, near Mountbellew in Galway, and had entered the convent of the Sisters of the Holy Ghost in San Antonio, Texas as a young teenager. This order of religious sisters operated a secondary school locally and had succeeded in recruiting quite a number of young girls from that area to join the order and pursue their mission of service to poor children in Texas via education. We happened to meet again by chance in late November 1975. We found that we had much in common and that we were on a similar faith journey and Church experience. She had decided that she was going to move on from religious life sometime in the following year. She left the convent in June 1976 and obtained her dispensation from religious vows. We became engaged and she obtained employment as a teacher with the Corpus Christi Independent School District. In July 1976, we both travelled home to Ireland. We met both families, shared our news and experienced their love, warmth and welcome. We are grateful to them all for their love, generosity and deep humanity which seemed to balance out their disappointment or concerns. In earlier decades of clerical domination, it was regarded as shameful for a family if a young man even left the seminary. Thankfully, by the mid-1970s, change was happening in Ireland and most Catholics had reached an understanding about the exodus of some priests and religious.

Joe and Maureen – Autumn 1976 – Corpus Christi

Maureen and I had become American citizens in earlier years and would always have the option of returning to live and work in America. However, we were both from large families and still had a hankering for Ireland and sharing in family events. In the light of the emerging threat that Rome would not grant my dispensation as long as I remained employed by the City of Corpus Christi and our joint calling back to Ireland, we reached a decision in November 1976 that we would leave Corpus Christi and return to Ireland around March 1977. In that case, it appeared doubly important that I try again to obtain the dispensation in preparation for possible marriage in Ireland in 1977. Many priests were leaving the priesthood and opted not to enter the dispensation process. In the light of our decision to return and marry in Ireland, I decided that I had to submit to all conditions in order to obtain the dispensation. Our good friend, Fr Pat Higgins introduced me to his brother Fr Michael Higgins who was a Canon Lawyer in the San Diego diocese. He had successfully processed many applications for dispensation and knew the exact requirements, formulae and contacts in the Curia. So he proposed a new plan of action and tore up my original letter of application for dispensation. Criticism of Rome or the Roman Catholic institution is anathema and is not allowed. Fr Michael was in possession of the complete template letter which might have some chance of getting a successful result in Rome. So, in November 1976, we devised a new letter, modelled on the template, which placed all possible blame on myself from earliest days and the weaknesses, faults and bad tendencies which rendered me suspect and unworthy of priesthood. By late November 1976, Fr Richard Shirley was the new Chancellor. He had completed a whole new questionnaire with me and accepted my newly composed letter of application. He noted our decision to leave the Corpus Christi area and return to Ireland. He was of the opinion that the newly-completed file would be quickly and successfully processed through Rome.

We returned to Ireland in March 1977 and we began the task of constructing a life together. By early summer there was no news from Corpus Christi or Rome. Further enquiries indicated that my dispensation file had vanished into limbo and was missing somewhere between Corpus Christi and Rome and that no time frame could be relied on for a decision. Accordingly, we moved ahead with our wedding plans. We married civilly in the Registrar's Office on Kildare Street on 12 August 1977 in a small private ceremony. The following day, in our rented accommodation at Highfield Park, Dundrum, my classmate and good friend Paddy Boyhan joined with us and the families in a private "station" Mass and unofficial wedding ceremony. From there, we adjourned to The Dalkey Island Hotel for traditional photography, reception, meal and dance together with family and friends. The dispensation finally came through in March 1978 and we exchanged vows once again in a small private "convalidation" ceremony at St Mark's Church in Springfield, Tallaght, on 15 April 1978. Yes – three times we exchanged vows and thankfully, we have been blessed through the years and have celebrated our 40th anniversary.

6

DUBLIN – 1977 TO DATE

St Attracta's Oratory, Meadowbrook, Dundrum, Dublin

I started work in June 1977 with Brady & Company beside the Four
Courts in Dublin. My job involved research in various public offices
such as the Land Registry, Registry of Deeds, Planning Departments
and Companies Office on all aspects of the title to any property in
Ireland. Law search companies serve solicitors and financial
institutions as part of the conveyancing process. I studied at night for
a diploma in legal studies from the College of Commerce in
Rathmines. My new work was a far cry from my original seminary
training, but I dedicated the next thirty plus years to that career path.
Those were also busy years of family life. Maureen and myself were
blessed with three sons and live in Dundrum, Dublin. Our estate is

Meadowbrook and has a very active residents association and tidy districts committee. The hard work and dedication over fifty years by a core group of about fifteen people of different religions in the above two groups has given us a great community spirit and a fine place to bring up a family. I have been active in helping to develop and maintain our estate with these people. We have won many prizes over the years from the county council.

Both Maureen and myself remain as practising Catholics in our local parish of St Attracta's, Meadowbrook, since 1978 and both of us continue to volunteer our service. I helped out with the parish newsletter, parish radio and Faith Friends programme. I served on the Parish Pastoral Council for some years. I enjoyed being part of a meet and greet ministry on Sundays as well as pastoral outreach to parish homes. Personal prayer remains important for us. I find it very helpful to give thanks, pray and celebrate daily mass with about eighty other mostly senior citizens and also to join with some of them in silent prayer and meditation during Exposition of the Blessed Sacrament.

This is a great parish community with plenty of lay people volunteering their talents in various parish ministries. We have a top-class school and excellent teachers. We have been blessed with a variety of fine priests and the warm presence of the Brigidine Sisters who have served as teachers and in various pastoral ministries. However, many of us who practice in the parish at this time are senior citizens. Over the past twenty years, we have witnessed the decline in attendance by many adults and most young people. As parents and grandparents, we are fully aware that some of our sons and daughters no longer walk the road of traditional church practice with us. They are good human beings and have not walked away from God. As parents we are concerned that the Christian message is obscured from people today behind patriarchal presentation and outdated clerical opinions on issues to do with sex and women together with a refusal to share power.

There is a shortage of priests countrywide and the remaining priests are overburdened. Instead of opening up the priesthood to women and married persons to address this shortage, the bishops have organised groups of parishes together into clusters. St Attracta's is now grouped or clustered with Holy Cross in Dundrum and St John's in Ballinteer. While we have been blessed by the part-time ministry of some Nigerian priests studying in Maynooth, there are now only two full-time priests to serve three large parishes. This process has happened everywhere and weakens the local parish community in terms of leadership, presence and coordination of pastoral care. People who have been taught and still believe that celebration of the Eucharist in local parishes is the treasure at the centre of Christian lives may now be denied that spiritual sustenance. Those same Catholic lay people can see that there is plenty of potential in every parish, that could provide priestly leadership, inspiration and pastoral care. As senior citizens who value families, we believe that the larger community unit of the local parish is very important for daily Christian inspiration as well as Sunday worship and key rituals. We believe that a vibrant local parish with an array of modern ministries provided by women and men can contribute enormously to the total well-being of individuals, the flourishing of families and the sense of belonging for all.

Alongside parish work, I also became involved with various Catholic reform groups. I would like to acknowledge the good example and inspiration provided for me over the years by several people. Soline Humbert together with her *Brothers and Sisters in Christ (BASIC)* group worked tirelessly for many decades to lobby for the ordination of women. Fr Michael Keane from Claremorris, Co Mayo was founder of the Knock Marriage Bureau and a great priest who cared deeply for the real needs of parishioners in the dioceses of

Tuam and Dublin. He was conscious of the need for urgent reform and spoke his truth firmly with courage. This did not endear him to superiors and the sheriff was used to oust him from the presbytery in 1981. Thankfully, he was reinstated and restored to public ministry in 2000. Fr Sean Fagan from Mullingar, a Marist priest and moral theologian, also saw the need for a new narrative and presentation. His prophetic writings did not find favour with authorities and were prohibited. Both of those men suffered unfairly at the hands of Catholic officialdom for daring to be honest and truthful. Sadly, both men are now deceased. I also want to acknowledge our indebtedness to five other priests still at this time being watched closely by Rome. They are Frs. Tony Flannery, Brian Darcy, Gerry Moloney, Iggy O'Donovan and Owen O'Sullivan. All of them have courageously and respectfully tried to raise questions in line with the needs and thinking of the people. All those men are prophetic priests and have been treated badly. Those of us who are not shackled by a vow of obedience have a duty to speak out with them and for the sake of our own integrity. In the wake of the recent revelations about treatment of mother and babies in the last century – for once and for all we have to question the Roman clerics and speak out as honest adult Catholics for justice in the most effective possible ways.

I also wish to remember and pay tribute to a dear friend named Terry Dosh from Minneapolis, USA, who died in 2016. I place him as representing that huge group of priests worldwide – more than 100,000 since the 1960's – who left the clerical state mainly because they wanted to marry. Terry had been a Benedictine monk. However, he joined the exodus of priests and married Millicent Adams in 1971. He never really left the priesthood but went about doing good and continued in various roles as a married priest activist. He served from 1984 to 1990 as the first National Coordinator in the United States of the *Corps of Reserved Priests United for Service (CORPUS).* It was set up as a support group for the

30,000 priests in America who had left the clerical state. Terry travelled to Ireland in 1986 and gave media interviews about the exodus from priesthood. CORPUS is now a faith community which affirms an expanded and inclusive priesthood rooted within a reformed and renewed Church.

I have continued to contribute to the debate and development in the Catholic church over the past forty years and have had numerous letters published in newspapers. In the late 1980s and early 1990s I took part with other former clerics and religious in numerous radio and television interviews and films. I have worked with the following Catholic groups since the eighties: *Pobal Dé* was a lay group which diligently sought implementation of Vatican II in regard to greater participation by lay people; *Leaven* was a support group for former clerics and religious which advocated an end to mandatory celibacy; *BASIC* was a devoted group of Catholic brothers and sisters in Christ who actively lobbied for women priests together with similar groups worldwide. The hardcore remnants of the above three groups are now assembled under the banner of *We Are Church Ireland* (WAC Ireland), of which I am a member. This tenacious and hardworking group of concerned Catholics is a member of the *International Movement We Are Church* (IMWAC). The group is working to end injustices in the Roman Catholic Church and is committed to the renewal of the Roman Catholic Church on the basis of the Second Vatican Council (1962–1965) and the theological spirit developed from it. Our monthly Dublin branch meeting has a speaker on some relevant topic followed by discussion and prayer. We use all possible methods to lobby Rome, the Papal Nuncio and the Bishops. We conduct surveys and collect signatures on various church issues. We engage with media via press releases, letters, radio and TV interviews and debates. Our Advent liturgy and various events are open to all and are advertised on our website and Facebook page. The group seeks to bring about informed dialogue among the People of God on the Five Aims/Objectives common to every national group within the *International Movement We Are Church*. Appendix A at the end of this book gives further details as regards *We Are Church Ireland* and suggestions for further action. Another lay organisation striving for reform is the *Association of Catholics in Ireland*. Further information is available from their website *acireland.ie*.

The *Association of Catholic Priests (Ireland)* (ACP) was established in 2011 by priests who were aware of the growing crisis. Tony Flannery, Brendan Hoban and Sean McDonagh provided early leadership. Those priests wished to have a forum and a voice for priests to reflect, discuss and comment on issues affecting the Irish Church and society today. It was an honour and an inspiration for me to have been asked in May 2012 to address an early public session of the ACP. Their public meetings in those years drew huge crowds. This association deserves our support.

The question is rightly asked of me as to whether I missed working as a priest or whether I would return to working as a priest if the opportunity arose. No, I didn't miss my earlier years as a seminarian and a priest. The marriage and family years have been a joy, a blessing and an ongoing challenge to be a bearer of faith, hope and love. Once married, I opted to do my best, despite faults and failings, in being a husband, father and a member of an extended family and parish. However, my involvement with reform groups as detailed in the above paragraphs was one way to exercise priestly ministry in accordance with my vocation. I have worked over the past two years to assemble my point of view in this book as a contribution to the Catholic conversation.

The difficulty facing all these groups over the years is that we have no vote within a monarchy centred in Rome and unelected leaders who have no ears to hear. In that situation of apparent powerlessness, the easiest option for most people is to give clergy and some church matters a very wide berth. It seems best to walk away towards life and involvement elsewhere in God's great world. It appears that the authoritarian faction within the Catholic Church wants us questioning Catholics to go away. No, we won't go away or become refugees. There has been more than enough splintering and sundering of the Christian family. To paraphrase sentiments expressed by the late Fr Joseph Dunn in *No Lions in the Hierarchy*, we won't jump off the Barque of Peter just because we disagree with some crew members who are slow to carry out repairs and change course. Catholic people in the developed world know that all human institutions are fallible and do wrong. We will continue to volunteer and serve within our local parishes and communities. The potential for society of a reformed, renewed and reunified Christian Church is immense. The issues involved in relation to women, equality, sexuality and democracy are hugely important. We, questioning Catholics, will no longer collude in the global maltreatment of women. Our clerical brothers in Rome and Armagh state that they were not aware decades ago of the seriousness of the issues to do with children and that they were on a learning curve. Catholic people, have to take a stand now and convince the slow learners that abuse of children, women, power, lay people and priests is totally wrong.

PART 2
CATHOLIC ISSUES
AND
DEBATES

7

CATHOLIC OPTIONS IN A CRISIS

In the Introduction, I outlined some elements of the growing crisis in the Catholic Church which is most evident in the developed world. Pope Francis' Letter of 20 August 2018 brought this into very sharp focus when he conceded that "we showed no care for the little ones; we abandoned them." He implicates all of us Catholics in the wrongdoing when he states, "we acknowledge as an ecclesial community that we were not where we should have been." It is a very serious matter if all of us Catholics are guilty just because of our baptism, presence and practice. Are innocent Catholics deemed to be at fault as long as we remain silent, deferential to clerics and unable to challenge the prevailing ecclesiastical culture in a meaningful way? Thankfully, Pope Francis has encouraged us all to say "no" to the abuse and an emphatic "no" to clericalism.

Catholic clericalism is a system or culture centred around an elite caste or religious hierarchy of celibate males who claim pre-eminence, special knowledge, privilege and power. This clerical culture is intrinsically disordered when it excludes women and proclaims that clerics are superior beings. It operates on outdated doctrines to do with sex, women and power. There are no checks and balances. The complicity of pious laity allows it to flourish. There is no real transparency or accountability. Any dissent or questioning is regarded as suspect and total obedience is demanded. Democratic or collegial structures are not allowed to develop within the Church institution.

I wish to draw attention to a scholarly study and a powerful book about the above issues. In *Child Sexual Abuse & The Catholic Church: Gender, Power and Organizational Culture*, Marie Keenan states that

the word clericalism is used to describe the situation where priests live in a hermetical world set apart from and set above the non-ordained members of the Catholic Church. The word is often used to describe the attitude that the clerical state is of divine origin and that it represents a higher calling than that of the lay state. It is a word often associated with a presumption of superiority.

Her final conclusion is, "that sexual abuse is inevitable given the meaning system that is taught by the Catholic Church and to which many priests adhere. The contradictions force failure and increase shame and a way of living that encourages sexually deviant behaviour." To the best of my knowledge, the above conclusion has not been challenged by the hierarchy. That statement, if true, is a very worrying assertion. That meaning system needs to be discussed and reviewed by Catholic people and poses an ongoing challenge to our honesty and integrity as practising Catholics. Those are the very deep roots from which the abuse will continue to happen in some cases and will require massive reform and change. Police vetting and child safeguarding agenda items at parish council meetings are a positive step but still only tinkering at the edges. Some practising Catholics may not want to know about serious structural defects and may pretend that there is no systemic fault. It is difficult enough to find language in regard to the core religious topics of God, Jesus Christ, Holy Spirit and Resurrection to reach potential believers today. However, that key task of evangelisation becomes almost impossible if the presentation is cloaked in clerical doctrines regarding sex, women and power. Die-hard defence of the indefensible will not enhance our credibility as parents trying to pass on the faith in God or as missionaries in the developed world.

It is right to shake the dust of clericalism out of our religious and spiritual lives. It is right to warmly invite clerics and priests to walk with us as equals in mission, service and ministry in a new era. There has been too much codology and nonsense. We need to end the silence and deference to clergy. We must stop putting clerics on pedestals. There must be straight-talking and active listening. There must be profound and enduring change.

For the moment, all of the issues as mentioned above remain unresolved. The outline of a massive program to act on the call by Pope Francis to say "no" to clericalism is nowhere in sight. In the meantime, the crisis deepens, and Catholics may pursue various options as follows:

1. FUNDAMENTAL OPTION

The best option available to all Catholics is to become better followers of Jesus Christ in our relationships, homes, parishes and workplaces. Based on faith, prayer and biblical study groups, we can become better followers by our loving way of life, respect and service to all plus action for justice in our Catholic Church and in our State. We can become a light to the world in co-operation with fellow Christians and all people as good Samaritans in feeding the hungry and caring for the poor, oppressed and homeless.

2. JOIN ANOTHER CHURCH OR RELIGION

Some Catholics have logically opted to join various Protestant churches or other religions. There are reports of significant movement in Latin America and Africa away from Catholicism to various evangelical Christian groups. I admire the Christian dedication, honesty and integrity of people I know in those churches. Their people have led the way to reform and progress. Centuries ago, their forefathers were appalled at the wrongdoing, deceit and corruption within the Roman Catholic Church. They were not listened to and were rejected out of hand. They were forced out of the Church in bloody wars. That was all wrong. Now, the various non-Catholic churches are available to us as sisters and brothers in Christ.

3. CIRCLE THE WAGONS

A small number of devout Catholics see no crisis whatsoever and seem happy enough to pay, pray and obey. They want to silence the survivors of abuse and may be unable to admit the failures of a faulty system. Some assert that there is no problem and that it is all fake news stirred up by elements of the media. Survivors who speak out are wrongly accused of bashing the Church when in fact they are challenging the wrongdoing arising from clericalism. A subset within this Catholic group wish to repeal and reverse Vatican II and proceed back in time to a perfect 19th century society with infallible clerical control. This group pride themselves on being anti-modern and counter-cultural.

4. MINIMAL INVOLVEMENT

A large number of Catholics are aware of the problems and have questions about the growing crisis. However, they sense that the clerical institution is irreformable and will not listen, share power, or change in their lifetimes. In a situation of powerlessness, those persons may attend mass on occasion but with minimal parish involvement.

5. WALK AWAY

A massive cohort of Catholics over the past fifty years have walked away from church attendance and parish involvement. This group is regarded as one of the largest "religious groups" in the United States at this time. They may still attend at Christmas and Easter as well as baptisms, weddings and funerals. Many continue to send their children to Catholic schools. It is perfectly understandable that many Catholic people have taken this option and that dignified people refuse to be insulted by having to accept elements of medieval clerical nonsense. When Catholics become convinced that clericalism will continue to rule supreme, it is one option to walk away with their presence, talents, time and money.

6. CATHOLIC REFORMERS

Some Catholic people continue to practice fully in parish but also speak out for change, reform and updating in the Catholic Church as per the spirit of Vatican II and conscious that Vatican III is urgently needed. This group wishes to end injustices in the Catholic Church. They are conscious of the massive potential in a reformed Catholic Church and a more united Christian family. This group desperately wants the gospel message at the core of our Catholic religion to be available to our children in new narrative, modern language and concepts, relevant ritual and updated structures which make sense to – and challenge – 21st century people. I count myself among this cohort. I admit that the task is very difficult and that it is much easier to walk away.

8

CHANGE IN THE ROMAN CATHOLIC CHURCH

Do not be afraid, O daughter of Zion: see, your king is coming, seated on a donkey's colt. (John 12, 15)

Defenders of the status quo often assert that the Roman Catholic Church is unchanging over two thousand years. They assert that it is a solid rock against reformers and can never admit error. They also state that it is not fickle and that it never bows to the winds of change or public opinion as some of the other Christian Churches are alleged to do. We have all been programmed that Rome has spoken and that is the end of the matter. Those of us who are senior citizens were brought up on the Penny Catechism. While there were undoubted essential religious truths contained therein and seemed set in stone, it failed in holding back the life force of change, reform and development in our world. People were programmed to parrot the answers but whether there was real evangelisation or education into the broader picture of historical religious realities is another matter.

However, change can happen, change has happened and change will happen.

As we have seen in Chapter 2 on the Second Vatican Council, change did happen on a whole range of very important issues. The issue of slavery is the clearest case of erroneous moral teaching over the centuries. As late as 1866, after slavery had been abolished in the USA, the Holy Office issued an instruction reaffirming the moral justification for slavery. *Rerum Novarum,* issued by Pope Leo XIII in 1891, began the process of changing the teaching on slavery which was finally corrected in the *Pastoral Constitution on the Church in the Modern World* in 1965.

In the decades since that Council, it appears that the minority group in Rome did not fully promulgate the teaching and proposed changes of Vatican II. During the pontificate of John Paul II (1978-2005), a major effort was made to restore aspects of the pre-Vatican II era and he produced *The Catechism of the Catholic Church.* This was the new official Catechism and was published in 1994. During his pontificate, dialogue and dissent was discouraged and theologians who advocated dialogue on contentious issues were heavily sanctioned. The pattern continued under Pope Benedict XVI. Catholics who have appealed for much-needed reform were authoritatively informed that nothing can change and that nothing will change on the key concerns to do with:

1. Ordination of women and equality for women in the ministry, governance and teaching office of the Church.
2. Contraception.
3. Compulsory or enforced celibacy.
4. Divorce and remarriage.
5. Homosexuality and other sexual issues.
6. Collegiality for bishops and active participation for all.

It is important for us to reflect on changes in doctrine that have happened over time. Most of us have little knowledge of the history of papal pronouncements or the evolution of Catholic dogma. In the course of my research for this book, I have come across many books dealing with reform, change and dissent. *Rome Has Spoken: A Guide to Forgotten Papal Statements, and How They Have Changed Through the Centuries*, by Maureen Fiedler and Linda Rabbens (editors), gives an overview and a crucial historical context about important issues on which there has been significant change or even reversal and U-turn. The book's chapter titles are as follows:

1.	Infallibility	10.	Women in the Church
2.	Primacy of Conscience	11.	Married Clergy
3.	Scriptural Interpretation	12.	Sexual Intimacy and Pleasure
4.	Religious Freedom	13.	Contraception
5.	Ecumenism	14.	Divorce and Remarriage
6.	The Jewish People	15.	Copernican Theory and Galileo
7.	Slavery	16.	Evolution
8.	Democracy in the Church	17.	War and Peace
9.	Theological Dissent	18.	Usury

Those are all very important issues with serious implications for the practice of our faith. However, none are the essential elements of our faith encounter with Jesus Christ. The sad truth is that our legitimate and understandable disagreement with clerical teaching on the above eighteen issues could have caused us to "walk away" and could have deprived us of the riches of parish community celebration.

I will just highlight two of the issues on which there has been change. Firstly, the official papal position over many centuries on anti-Semitism gave powerful religious support to the prevailing attitude towards Jewish people. The official magisterium only changed its position around the time of Vatican II, decades after millions had perished. Secondly, on usury - the lending of money at interest - the official church magisterium condemned the practice until around the early 19th century. Since 1917, Canon Law requires interest-taking as a mandatory responsibility for those administering Church assets. Changed economic realities and developed under-standing of money led to a change of teaching on a moral issue which you could argue is of greater importance in the everyday lives of people than some of the sexual issues. However, you will still be told that women can never be ordained.

The book shows that change has happened over the centuries. It took a long time to partially acknowledge that Galileo was right and had been cruelly wronged by the Roman Catholic authorities. It can be a terribly difficult Christian challenge to admit ' mistakes and that change must happen. I get very annoyed with clerics or traditionalists who have no answer for the reasonable calls for reform except the cynical retort that of course change may happen in a thousand years. They boast that the Church moves slowly. That is not good enough for people in the 21st century.

YOU CAN DISAGREE

All exhortations in the past (and present) about the constancy of Church doctrine are usually accompanied by the admonition that dissent will not be tolerated from papal teachings. If you do dare to question or seek dialogue you will be shown the exit with good riddance. We'd prefer not to become refugees or exiles from our faith family. The Catholic Church should be centred on Jesus Christ and is not at its best as a monarchy. Away from medieval tyrants and dictators in some countries, most of us are blessed to have progressed into a democratic world. Democracy is not a perfect system, but it is among the best we know. In our democratic world, you cannot tell a person with a dissenting viewpoint to leave the country.

Why You Can Disagree and Remain a Faithful Catholic by Philip Kaufman, is an excellent book which presents the case and place for disagreement and dissent on various moral issues. The author asserts that Catholics have a right to be aware of a broad range of Catholic information and theological opinions as well as the official teaching from Rome. The official teaching has come from a small cohort of men who claim special power. It could represent an ancient school of thought. It is possible that the official teaching could have arisen out of a celibate psychosis or sexual resentment and envy. It may not have been leavened by the good sense and wisdom of all the bishops. Teaching fails to be teaching when it is not accepted by those taught. Clerical teaching on papal infallibility was proclaimed in 1870 in turbulent circumstances. I question its value and consider it an obstacle to reunion. It is important to note that only two doctrines have been promoted as infallible: one relating to the Immaculate Conception and the other, the Assumption of Our Lady. Accordingly, Catholics have a right to know that no Church teaching on moral issues has been defined and to be aware of the options when genuine doubt exists. There is serious dissent by qualified theologians from the official magisterium on several moral issues. Unanimous and total acceptance of the birth control encyclical in 1968 was not forthcoming from all the bishops' conferences worldwide. There was a broad range of nuanced response and obsequious deference. All of this information should be a valid and available source for the laity in the formation of a fully informed and enlightened conscience.

The above book deals in detail with the issues of birth control, divorce and remarriage. It also delves into very important topics such as democracy in the Church, election of bishops, subordination of the laity, the struggle for power and intercommunion. I think this book could be especially helpful for any Catholics constrained by narrow clerical tradition or Catholics who have "fallen away" because of difficulties with official teaching.

9

ORDINATION OF WOMEN

You did not choose me, but I chose you to go and bear fruit that will last.

John 15, 16

It is becoming increasingly obvious to me that the Church cannot fly on one male wing. It is disheartening to see only male celebrants at community masses with women excluded from leadership and governance. The traditionalists may justify this sexist and unfair treatment through theological reasonings or absolute codology. They may continue to defend the indefensible. However, more and more people are realising that the clerical position on these matters is nonsensical and unjust and are walking away. As a result, the riches at the core of our Catholic parish worship, celebration of Sacraments and social work may be obscured or denied to them.

If we are to say "no" to clericalism, then the old models of priesthood must be abandoned. I am a proponent of ordination of women into a totally reformed ministry for the 21st century which takes full account of the priesthood of all the baptised and equal participation by all in the mission of Jesus Christ. Women must have their equal role in leadership, governance, ministry and formation of a new narrative.

In this chapter, I attempt to set out some basic responses to the main arguments as presented by those who are opposed to the ordination of women.

TRADITION

Clerics continue to equate the hierarchy with the Catholic Church when in fact they are only a part of it. It is true to say that the constant tradition of this ancien régime is opposed to the ordination of women. That clerical tradition is based on the suppression of women by celibates. The Church Fathers were people of their time and place. They regarded women as inferior to men, disobedient daughters of Eve and sources of temptation. The apostles were influenced by pre-Christian sects with negative teachings about women and sexuality. There was an ancient taboo against menstrual blood and the blood of childbirth. Aspects of this negative approach to women continued with the rite of "Churching" of women post-childbirth up to the 1960s. Women had to be veiled and silent. They couldn't serve at the altar as per the 1917 Code of Canon Law. Women were also forbidden to sing in choir or to be within the altar rails up to the 1950s. In 1980, Pope John Paul II ordered that women couldn't serve at the altar. Uta Ranke-Heinemann in her book *Eunuchs for the Kingdom of Heaven: Women, Sexuality and the Catholic Church* clearly articulates the contempt for sex and women which saturated the thinking of Church Fathers and which still lies at the root of papal opposition to artificial contraception and ordination of women.

Inter Insigniores on the Question of the Admission of Women to the Ministerial Priesthood, issued in 1976 by the Sacred Congregation for the Doctrine of the Faith and approved by Pope Paul VI together with *Ordinatio Sacerdotalis* issued by Pope John Paul II in 1994, are the two key declarations in the past fifty years concerning the ordination of women. Both documents were formulated by members of the hierarchy. All were trained in the traditions of the Church Fathers with all the negative baggage about women as outlined above. The hierarchy see men and priests as supreme and foremost within the community. The documents were not formulated by lay women and men enriched by Vatican II and having reached new awareness of civil rights, human rights, justice, equality and discrimination. The arguments in the above documents did not really convince adults decades ago. In the light of developments in recent decades, the arguments as presented are dubious indeed.

It is right to ask questions and demand good answers. Who formulated the catechism or Canon Law? Who approved the Scriptures as we have it today from among various oral traditions and agendas? Which apostle laid the foundations for anti-Semitism or approved of slavery? Who controlled or developed the tradition? Is the tradition based on the wisdom of the People of God or is it a clerical opinion? In the absence of a divine blueprint, the simple answer is that all are man-made and developed over time in different cultures to meet changing needs. As such, all those traditions, theologies, rules and laws are limited, deficient, fallible and subject to reform.

Men have firmly stated in the past that woman's place was in the home and that she had absolutely no right to vote or participate in the public realm. Men said that women couldn't serve on juries. Clerics who assert that women cannot be ordained are following the same sexist traditions. Worse still, they blame Jesus for their restrictions on women. I am glad that this line of argument in regard to the vote and other issues was defeated over one hundred years ago. Now it is time for change in the Church.

There are some great traditions to which we should cling. Examples include: having all things in common, turning the other cheek, loving enemies, feeding the hungry, treating your fellow man as yourself, etc. However, there are lots of ignoble traditions which we should discard as quickly as possible such as: racism, fascism, misogyny, anti-Semitism, sexism, Crusades, Inquisition. We are all only too well aware of groups in the Middle East and Africa who cling grimly to their tradition within which they restrict, hamper and handicap women. As Catholics, we do not wish to hang on to any outdated traditions. We know that as a Christian Church we should be out front giving good example rather than being dragged reluctantly out of the Middle Ages to grant equality for women.

The Gospel of Mark (7:1-8,14-15,21-23), details an encounter between Jesus and his regular opponents among the Scribes and Pharisees. Those people were extremely loyal to traditions and observances of the elders in regard to washing elbows, sprinkling cups and eating food. Jesus got annoyed with their spying, pettiness and legalism. He shouted,

> *it was of you hypocrites that Isaiah so rightly prophesied in this passage of Scripture 'this people honours me only with lip service while their hearts are far from me. The worship they offer me is worthless, the doctrines they teach are human regulations.' You put aside the commandment of God to cling to human traditions.*

This reading applies powerfully to the clerical traditions within the Roman Church today. The purely man-made regulations suppressing women have become more important than the celebration of Eucharist and pastoral care.

SCRIPTURE, JESUS AND THE LAST SUPPER

"Last Supper", by Bohdan Piasecki

The simplistic story presented by Church Fathers was that Jesus brought twelve apostles into an upper room for an elite ordination ceremony. Everybody else, including his mother, were excluded. This is one foundation for the tradition of a male-only priesthood. In 1976, after much research, the Pontifical Biblical Commission reported that *it could find no support* for this position on the basis of biblical evidence alone. Those scholars had access for decades to modern methods of biblical exegesis or decoding. The scholars had moved beyond literal reading of the old texts. They were equipped to produce nuanced interpretation rather than simple stories for children. Their report was not to the liking of Pope Paul VI or the Roman Curia since it did not support the official line. Accordingly, the report was not made public and was omitted from the Vatican website.

The historical story appears more complex. It is presented in the context of a Passover Meal including women and children. All were invited to do this in memory of Him as disciples and apostles. It was not an ordination ceremony. The priestly caste in our Roman Church only emerged from 400AD approx. onwards. It gradually evolved and was modelled on other religions and Roman imperial practice. The disciples of Jesus Christ met in family homes in the early centuries. Women and men presided at the meals. Women served as deacons for hundreds of years. They all shared bread and wine and encountered the Risen Christ. They healed and helped and shared in community. They all took part in decisions and all joined in the selection of servant leaders. However, the prevailing culture of the time was patriarchal and favoured suppression of women. Slowly, the early Christian communities succumbed to that control and the professional caste of priests emerged in the centuries after the Christian religion became the official sanctioned religion of the Roman Empire in 315.

The following quote from *No Lions in the Hierarchy* by Joseph Dunn expresses the reality of that time:

> *The customs and attitudes of the times made it difficult to appoint women as apostles. To have women leave their homes and roam the world preaching, founding or governing churches was not a real option in the circumstances of the time. But, times have changed.*

So, Jesus as a Jewish man probably chose twelve men to replace the Twelve Tribal Fathers of Israel as a realistic foundation option. In the cultural context of that time, men emerged as the chosen ones in control. The evolving Christian community, as guided by the Holy Spirit, later moved to incorporate Gentiles in the salvation plan. This is a good example of something Jesus did *not do* at the Last Supper. Jesus did not include any Gentiles at the Last Supper. Yet, we are all glad today that Paul and the early community were inspired to confront Peter and insisted that Gentiles were indeed included in the plan of salvation. There are lots of things that Jesus did *not do* at the Last Supper but which we now incorporate in the church today. Jesus did not have any Irish, Italians, Argentinians or black people at the Last Supper, yet we do not exclude them. Change, development, exodus and evolution seems to be a natural law. It is way past time to ordain women who were indeed present as disciples at the Last Supper.

Some further questions to pose are as follows. What was the attitude of Jesus and the Apostles at the Last Supper towards the Vatican Bank or the garb of cardinals within the splendour of the Vatican? What was the recommended practice by Jesus and the Apostles at the Last Supper in regard to the cover-up of crimes and the refusal to cooperate with civil authorities?

JESUS WAS A MAN. A WOMAN CANNOT IMAGE THE MALE JESUS

The aforementioned document, *Inter Insigniores,* asserts strongly that Catholic priesthood is for males only. It states repeatedly that Christ was and is a man. Thereby, they seem to assert that God in Christ the man is forever male. I strongly question that clerical statement that the Risen Christ is a flesh and blood man like me in our world today. Today, however, the Holy Spirit appears to be leading spiritual writers and theologians towards language and concepts about God being beyond male and female categories. It is true that the historical Jesus was a man. The Risen Christ is a different reality and in a heavenly condition beyond male or female. Women are not able to present a natural resemblance to Jesus the Galilean. However, there is no doubt, but that Christ-like women can image or represent the Risen Lord as priests and servant leaders. His mission was to be in solidarity with all humankind. Jesus pronounced that we are all beloved daughters and sons of God. He proclaimed that insight and ran into serious trouble with the religious authorities.

In all four Gospels, Mary of Magdala was the first witness to the most important event in Christianity, namely the Resurrection of Jesus Christ. On foot of this experience, Mary of Magdala became the apostle to the apostles. Then all of them together experienced the presence of the Risen Christ and a Holy Spirit sending them forth with a message of new life. All of us are baptised as priests, prophets and kings into the new life of the Risen Christ. Paul in his letter to the Galatians (Gal 3: 27 – 28) seems to sum up the new reality very well, "All baptised in Christ, you have all clothed yourselves in Christ, and there are no more distinctions between Jew and Greek, slave and free, male and female, but all of you are one in Christ Jesus."

The author Angela Hanley raises the following question in her highly relevant book *Whose A la Carte Menu?*

Why decide on maleness as a norm? Why not ethnicity? Jesus was a Jew, through and through – it was as a Jew that he preached. Why not stipulate that only Palestinian Christians can be priests? It makes just as much sense.

If there emerges definitive biblical, sociological or theological proof that maleness is intrinsic to priesthood, then it will be time for us Christians to abandon pagan priesthood and move beyond ordination to a discipleship of equals in Christ.

POPE JOHN PAUL II HAS DECLARED DEFINITIVELY THAT WOMEN CANNOT BE ORDAINED

If I have the gift of prophecy and can fathom, all mysteries and all knowledge, and if I have a faith that can move mountains, but have not love, I am nothing.
1 Co 13, 2

91

Pope John Paul II in *Ordinatio Sacerdotalis* unilaterally declared that there was a scriptural basis for women's exclusion from ordination. Notwithstanding the fact that he was not a bibilical scholar, *Ordinatio Sacerdotalis* also ran counter to the Pontifical Biblical Commission in 1976. To the best of my knowledge, the Pope had not consulted the College of Bishops worldwide or the Synod of Bishops on this hugely important issue. It appears to me that he should have done so in accordance with the new emphasis on collegiality in the Vatican II document *Constitution on the Church*. He also asserted that the exclusion of women from orders was to be definitively held. This was an attempt to imbue the notion of infallibility into his statement even though it did not meet the criteria for such a declaration. He also decreed that the matter was closed for further discussion. It was a sure sign that his back up arguments were very weak and that the old Thomistic foundations for this clerical suppression of women were no longer valid.

The idea of absolute obedience and uncritical loyalty to any monarch probably ended in the free world shortly after World War II. The defence of absolute obedience to orders did not hold up for Adolf Eichmann in the Nuremberg trials. Many Catholics worldwide are not impressed with the loyal obedience of bishops worldwide to the Vatican directives favouring the institution over children. Many Catholics today are becoming aware that popes, bishops and priests are indeed fallible human beings like all of us. The revelations over the past decades about cover-up under official Roman orders has begun to open our eyes in regard to absolute obedience to any monarch. Pius XI in his 1931 *Encyclical on Christian Education* solemnly declared that "coeducation (girls and boys together) is erroneous and pernicious, and often based on naturalism which denies original sin." I think most Catholics today have quietly moved on beyond that papal statement.

"IT DIDN'T WORK FOR THE PROTESTANTS"

In terms of Church history, it is far too early to make the above statement with any semblance of truth or definitive proof. The subtext within the above assertion is that the Protestants have got it wrong again regarding the ordination of women. This blinkered assertion states that the number of practising Protestants in England and Ireland is dropping even though they have had ordination of women for decades. The argument may not be accurate from a wider perspective. Protestant congregations might appear to be dropping in England, Ireland and Europe. However, an article in *The Economist* stated as follows:

> *Protestantism continues to change lives today; indeed, over the recent decades the number of its adherents has grown substantially; more than 40% of Guatemala's population is now Protestant. Its story is a microcosm of a broader "Protestant awakening" across Latin America and the developing world. According to the Pew Research Centre, Protestants currently make up slightly less than 40% of the world's 2.3 billion Christians. The United States is home to some 150 million Protestants, the largest number in any country. Today Europe accounts for only 13% of the world's Protestants. The faith's home is the developing world. Nigeria has more than twice as many Protestants as Germany. More than 80 million Chinese have embraced the faith in the past 40 years. (4 - 10 November 2017)*

If ordination of women is the right and just path to follow, then all of us Christians together should pursue the new approach. Nobody claims that this is the total answer to all the complex problems with evangelisation in the modern world. However, it is a step in the right direction. All of us Christians, East and West, North and South need to unite and cooperate in our encounter with Jesus Christ. It is time to say yes – yes to truth and justice and forgiveness and love and reconciliation. It is time to stop tribal squabbles and to work together to build up the Kingdom of God. It is time for a united Christian Church to lead the whole world away from misogyny, patriarchy and injustice to women.

WOMEN ARE DIFFERENT FROM MEN BUT COMPLEMENTARY

Some of our companions went to the tomb and found everything exactly as the women had reported, but of him they saw nothing.   Luke 24, 24

Complementarianism is a male theological thesis held by some in Christianity, Judaism and Islam, that men and women have different but complementary roles and responsibilities in marriage, family life, religious leadership and elsewhere. A key conclusion of this thesis is that those different roles preclude women from leadership, authority, formulation of doctrine, priesthood and governance. Women can be mothers in the home and play minor roles elsewhere. Men can be fathers, priests, rulers and lawmakers. Male hegemony is part and parcel of the Bible stories. Eve was disobedient and accordingly women are adjudged ill-suited for ruling and authority. Based on a clerical interpretation of certain biblical passages, Pope John Paul II proclaimed the primary headship of men and helpmate roles for women. While sounding benevolent, the official hierarchical position on complementarity firmly restricts women to minor roles. The bottom line is that while women may assist in the decision-making process, the ultimate authority for the decision in home, family or church is for the male alone. The important point to remember is that complementarianism is a male construct from an old world. Today, we are slowly moving forward out of slavery, domination and oppression. It appears that many people are beginning to reject the male chauvinist bias that men are of significantly greater value than women. I favour the egalitarian position that authority and responsibility in marriage, family, religion and elsewhere should be equally available to women and men.

The above argument by clerics about "different but complementary" is a version of the old segregation/apartheid policy as implemented centuries ago in South Africa and the Deep South, USA. The public policies of slavery and racism were deeply embedded in those regimes. It would have been stated that blacks and whites are different but the subtext for those in control was that blacks were inferior. It was decreed that there should be separate restaurants, roles, beaches and toilets for different races. Within those oppressive regimes, blacks and whites could complement themselves as slaves and masters. Thankfully, that line of argument was defeated in the civil rights and anti-apartheid struggles of the last century. The difficult process of integration, power-sharing and cooperation is moving slowly forward this time centred on the common humanity of blacks, whites and coloureds.

I think that Catholics today are not fooled by the paternalistic notion of complementary roles. All the polls in recent decades in Ireland show that a large majority of Catholics favour ordination of women and an egalitarian approach. Ordination of women and integration into ministry needs to happen now. Catholic clericalism today is intrinsically disordered because the crucial priestly talents of women have been deliberately excluded.

GOD ALONE GIVES THE VOCATION – NO ONE HAS A RIGHT OR ENTITLEMENT

The talents and call to loving service come from God to all human beings and is not restricted to males. You could argue that no one has a right to ordination, but how is it that only men can present themselves? Why is it that only men control entry to the seminaries? A group of very fallible men have pursued a doctrine of excluding women from ministry. Some Catholic women have experienced the call from God to priesthood but found the road blocked by holy men. Away from any divine intervention, it was always the men on the ground who admitted, approved, trained and ordained an all-male priesthood. Did God make some terrible mistake in giving vocations to some clerical paedophiles and rapists? Did Jesus Christ and the Holy Spirit mistakenly call some priests and bishops to anti-Christian behaviour? Of course not. The original policy of suppression and the mistakes were all made by men.

The People of God worldwide have not been consulted on the matter of the ordination of women. The People of God have not been asked for wisdom and consensus. Just as in the cases of slavery and anti-Semitism, it took a long time to reach awareness that those teachings were wrong. People today are coming to an awareness of the dignity and calling of all human beings. All of us are called by God to active participation in the mission of Jesus Christ. It is unjust for clerics to claim a divine mandate to shut the doors against women going forward for selection, election and ordination.

HOPE FOR THE FUTURE

Postcard commissioned by BASIC in 2000 promoting the ordination of women.

The Angelus prayer reminds us that God chose a woman to make Jesus present in the flesh in our world. Jesus loved and respected women. Jesus was not suspicious of women. Jesus was not hostile towards women. Jesus did not see women as unholy, unclean, unworthy or inferior. Jesus treated women as equals and dined with them. The following quotation from *Catholicism* by Richard McBrien is apt, "in striking contrast to the contemporary usages of the Jewish world, Jesus surrounded himself with women who followed him and served him (Luke 8: 2 – 3; Luke 10: 38 – 42)." Jesus raised eyebrows even among his own followers when he shared water and wisdom with the woman at the well. Women were his disciples and were present at the Last Supper. Women remained at the foot of the Cross when men ran away. The New Testament includes many passages depicting women as leaders in early Christianity.

Women can be presidents or prime ministers. We have female judges, cabinet ministers and women contributing their unique talent and genius in all fields. Women can be Doctors of the Church. They can be saints or mystics or abbesses or spiritual directors. Why not priests? Women can be Christ-like servant leaders of the Catholic parish community or diocese or the Universal Church. They can gather us in prayer, thanksgiving, remembrance and encounter with the Risen Christ. Women can proclaim the Word of God and reveal valuable new insights from their crucial female perspective. They can provide rich spiritual nourishment in different ways. Their input will help to rectify the centuries long deficiencies in our spiritual lives. They can present the challenge of the amazing Gospel message and help to inspire us as disciples to build up the Kingdom of God. Women can celebrate wholeness and holiness the same as men. Women can be stewards of the mysteries of God the same as men. Women and men in service as priests are absolutely essential for spiritual wellbeing and Catholic wholeness.

It is probably not widely known that women have been ordained to the Roman Catholic priesthood. In *Out of the Depths: The Story of Ludmila Javorova, Ordained Roman Catholic Priest*, Miriam Winter tells the true story of a woman who was ordained a priest in the underground church of Communist Czechoslovakia on 28 December 1970 by Bishop Felix Davidek. Javarova was the Vicar-General of a major branch of the underground Czech Church for twenty years and ministered in dangerous circumstances with about five other women priests. The Iron Curtain collapsed in 1990 and she was forced by Rome to end her priestly ministry. The female clandestine priest was no longer needed, and the short-lived phenomenon of Catholic women priests was disappeared.

However, that is not the end of the story. Over the past decades, more than two hundred Catholic women have been ordained priests in Europe and the USA by three unnamed Roman Catholic bishops who decided to challenge the prevailing clerical culture. Those validly ordained bishops believed that the time had come for the ordination of women. In secret, they ordained women as priests. Later, they ordained some of the women as bishops to remove the ongoing need for clandestine participation of the three male bishops. The *Roman Catholic Women Priests* (RCWP) movement began in 2002 with the ordination of seven women on the Danube river. *Women Find a Way* by the authors Elsie McGrath, Ida Raming and Bridget Mary Meehan, documents the history of the movement. Bridget Mary Meehan, from Rathdowney Co Laois, has lived in the USA for many years. She was ordained a priest in the first US ordination in Pittsburgh in July 2006. Later, she was ordained a bishop in Santa Barbara, California, in April 2009. She is now a member of the pastoral team at Mary Mother of Jesus Inclusive Catholic Community in Sarasota, Florida. Catholic communities in Virginia and Florida approve her ordination and confirm her in ministry. She leads those groups in celebration of the Eucharist and action for justice. She visits Ireland each summer and has been interviewed on media. Together with other Catholic reformers, I concelebrated a Eucharist with her in RTE some years ago as part of a religious broadcast. She is a courageous and articulate woman. Together with her female priest colleagues, they are providing a new model of ministry, leadership and pastoral care. Slowly but surely, I pray that the Roman Catholic Women Priests movement will flourish and reveal different religious riches. Bishop Meehan would like to meet Irish Catholic women who feel called to priesthood and who want to be the change. Contact details are contained in the bibliography. Thankfully, a number of priests have taken a stand on the importance and urgency of this issue of equality for women. They have taken a big risk and have endured punishment and some, excommunication. We need to protest at this inquisition and must support those priests and theologians in any way we can.

It is true to say that there has been a small measure of progress since Vatican II regarding the role of women in parishes. We have female Ministers of the Eucharist and Readers. We have altar girls as well as female pastoral workers. Many women have obtained qualifications and degrees in theology, spirituality, chaplaincy and pastoral care. We have a growing cadre of female chaplains providing excellent ministry in our hospitals. They accompany people of all faiths and none. They can preside at funeral rituals and at Services of Word and Holy Communion. Sadly, however, despite the shortage of ordained male priests, those chaplains are not allowed to administer the Sacrament of the Sick. This is restricted to ordained males only.

Injustice and maltreatment of women is a tragic sickness which pervades society. It is deeply rooted in misogyny and sexism. The Rape Crisis Centres and the women's shelters tell tragic stories to add to the everyday realities of workplace harassment. Sadly, the tradition of treating women badly persists in all arrogant hierarchies. Unfortunately, the dominant clerical tradition within Catholicism of suppression of women has been a major contributor to the ongoing disease. The ordination of women is a crucial pro-justice issue. It is time for all of us together, lay people, priests, religious and bishops to work towards a wholesome new tradition of justice and ordination for women.

In this chapter on a complex topic of huge importance, I only touch on some themes and direct you to a more comprehensive treatment of the subject by the following authors in the bibliography: Mary Malone, John Wijngaards, Sharon Tighe-Mooney, Jimmy Carter, Lavinia Byrne and Joan Chittester.

10

OBEDIENT CATHOLICS = PERFECT CATHOLICS?

According to the Gospel of Matthew, the test of being a perfect Catholic appears to centre on selling everything that you own, giving the proceeds to the poor and following Jesus. However, today, some traditionalists define it as absolute obedience to hierarchical authorities and total acceptance of their menu. They would say that you cannot dissent in any way from their extensive list of rules, regulations, rituals, traditions and medieval teachings. Catholics who try to discern between the crucial gospel message and the much less important clerical teachings are met with withering condemnation from Church Fathers. Catholics who attempt to reconcile their faith and clerical teaching with scientific discoveries or new knowledge are scorned. That medieval approach is not acceptable today. There should be room in the Catholic Church for regional diversity and freedom in debatable matters. Slavish obedience is not always virtuous. The civil rights struggles demonstrated that civil disobedience helped to dismantle evil systems.

Peter preached in the Acts of the Apostles that only Jewish people could become Christians and that all males must be circumcised. Thankfully, Paul and others spoke out and questioned this opinion. The limited Petrine menu was subsequently broadened to include all Gentiles. The Fathers had also decided that slavery was good for the soul and that rewards would be in Heaven. It was in the holy books as spoken, written and assembled by the patriarchs. Thankfully, after long centuries, the Holy Spirit led us away from slavery and human rights appeared on a new menu.

The splendour of Empire and Rome and the Vatican Bank and wealth and property and vestments and titles seems an "a la carte" choice by men or a very long way removed from the humble Jesus and gospels program – nowhere to lay his head – all things in common – carry no purse or haversack. The Crusades, Inquisition, and religious wars seem to be very "a la carte" by the authorities or a very long way from the goodness and gentleness of Jesus and the Gospels. The supreme religious leaders had decided a long time ago that the Jews were "Jesus killers" and that they must be set apart in a ghetto in the Middle Ages. That all resulted in horror. However, you would be vilified as a disobedient Catholic for picking and choosing against that doctrine in the Middle Ages.

Do real, orthodox and traditionalist Catholics still hold on to the papal teaching from many centuries ago that there was no salvation outside the Roman Catholic Church and that all others were doomed to hell? The world moved on and the bishops at Vatican II changed that dangerous doctrine. Are we to accept that your mark as a Catholic is uncritical acceptance of any decree by Pope or Curia even if they state that child abuse must be covered up? Are you one-hundred per cent Catholic only if you accept that the Roman Church is above the law and that it should not cooperate with civil authorities? Are you a perfect Catholic only if you accept that the sun revolves around the earth and that the Inquisition was the right way to deal with people who asked questions? Was Jesus disobedient when he healed on the Sabbath and protected the woman caught in adultery? The above examples and lots of others over the course of history show the need for some teachings to be questioned. In any State or institution where a dictator or monarch refuses to listen to the cries for reform, only damage, destruction and death results. Absolute obedience and loyalty to a dictator were features of bad regimes in the past. Understandably, we are suspicious today of such systems which may demand blind obedience as the top virtue.

Children may be baptised, confirmed and indoctrinated. Devout persons may remain obedient and silent out of deference or fear. Adults with more knowledge and experience naturally raise questions as part of their religious development. When church reformers raise questions about systemic problems, they can be dismissed by the hierarchy as disobedient people. They may be denigrated as "lukewarm" or "a la carte" Catholics in order to avoid dealing with the obvious problems. As a result, the crisis deepens to the detriment of all. It appears to me that our mark as Catholics should be the fact that we are loving and joyful disciples of Jesus Christ.

COUNTER-CULTURAL CATHOLICS

Some Catholics proclaim that another mark of being a Catholic is that the Church community must be counter-cultural. That is the code word today for the papal policies of anti-modernism in the late 19th and early 20th century. The Second Vatican Council moved beyond that outdated position, encouraged us to read the "signs of the times" and to actively participate in building up the Kingdom of God today. We do not wish to live in the past. The secular West is not bad. It has problems and difficulties just like East, South and North. God remains present everywhere including the West. People in the world today have learned, advanced, developed and grown up. They continue to search for God in language, concepts and narrative that make sense to them today.

I admit that there is a strong argument that Jesus Christ challenges our selfish preoccupations and greed. He challenges us to work with others for the common good. He asked us to keep the commandments and to love God and neighbour. He challenges us to feed the hungry and to forgive seventy times seven. He spoke about turning the other cheek. That is an extremely difficult challenge for us all.

However, it appears to me that the counter-cultural card can be overplayed and could sometimes stray into nonsense. It all depends on whether you still hold that progress, development and the modern world is all bad. There are undoubted problems and evil behaviour in the modern world. However, there is much good in global cultural trends over the past centuries. We have progressed from serfdom and slavery towards greater freedom as well as human rights. It seems good to move towards full civil rights and justice for all people; to move away from the horrendous anti-Semitism of earlier centuries; to move away from homophobia towards respect for diversity and positive celebration of our sexuality. The cultural trend towards respect, equality and justice for women appears to me as a wonderful step on the Exodus journey. In this context, the insistence that males alone have the potential for priesthood rests on very unsound and fragile foundations. A Catholic counter-cultural position against equality and justice for women seems like madness to me.

11

WHY SHOULDN'T THE CHURCH BE DEMOCRATIC?

The majority of the world's countries are now governed by democratic regimes, defined as systems with citizen political participation, effective checks and balances, and a guarantee of civil liberties. Humanity over many centuries paid a huge price in blood, sweat and tears in the struggle for respect, liberty and equality. Most of us value our right to vote, select our governments and play an equal part with others in our country. We have moved on from the Roman Empire. Unfortunately, elements of its mentality and structures have remained in the Roman Catholic Church. We have moved on from the various cruel, violent and unjust colonial empires. There are examples today of modern empires engaging in war and injustice in pursuit of resources. There are countries living under tyranny and versions of the communist systems still out there show scant regard for the individual or human rights. However, the God of Exodus seems to be leading people slowly and gradually out of the slavery of past millennia into more democratic government systems. Democracy is not perfect and has presented some serious issues in recent years. However, new systems of checks and balances can be devised and it can always be improved. Largely, it is true to say that people in more developed parts of the world favour democracy and over imperial or colonial rule.

However, the unfortunate fact is that structures, systems and mentality at the Roman centre of the institutional Catholic Church have not been amended in line with changes made over centuries. Whilst the Second Vatican Council was a marvellous attempt at reform, sadly the small minority on all votes in the Council and two reactionary Popes somehow hampered progress contributing to the current crisis. Accordingly, democratic Catholic people today will rightly and increasingly walk away from an institution which defines itself as a monarchy with central control and which steadfastly refuses to share power with bishops, priests and lay people. This is a tragedy for individuals and local parish communities. It seems very difficult to evangelise today in the language of monarchy, hierarchy, patriarchy, central control and the refusal to share power.

We are conscious since Vatican II of the Church as a communion of people baptised into Jesus Christ and guided by the Holy Spirit of Love as a discipleship of equals. We accept that imperial structures and systems inevitably developed in the Catholic Church in the time of the Roman Empire. That time is long past. Catholic people need to speak out in favour of democratic or collegial systems which we consider right today and very much in accordance with the Gospel texts.

Pre-Vatican II clerical doctrine stressed for Catholics that the Roman Catholic Church can only be a monarchy which claims infallible answers and superior knowledge. An example of that programming from the past was the encyclical *Vehementer* by Pius X in 1906. He stated that the Church is essentially an unequal society of pastors and flock and that the one duty of the multitude as a docile flock is to follow the pastors. So, if we are not aware of the fact that Vatican II significantly improved on that papal teaching, then we may be operating as programmed to nod in agreement at anything a Pope or bishop says. Most of us do not have the perspective in regard to church history and may not have the knowledge to assert that things can be different and should be different.

A Democratic Church: The Reconstruction of Roman Catholicism by Eugene Bianchi and Rosemary Ruether (editors), is a hugely important book dealing with the topic of democracy in the Church. The following quotation captures the essence of the ongoing conversation about the issue:

Whenever groups of Catholics attempt to assert rights of popular decision-making in the church, it is common for bishops to declare, 'the church is not a democracy.' While this may be an accurate factual statement about the church today, the assumptions that it is an accurate historical statement or a biblically and theologically normative statement needs to be challenged. The essential question is 'why shouldn't the church be democratic?' Those who make such statements assume that the Roman Catholic Church historically has always possessed a centralised monarchical and hierarchical form of government and that this government was given to it by Jesus Christ. It is therefore divinely mandated and unchangeable. It is the intention of this book to challenge this set of assumptions, to show that democratic elements have always existed in the past in certain aspects of church government, and that democratic polity suits the theological meaning of the church as a redemptive society better than does monarchical hierarchy.

The book is a compilation from various scholars dealing with the topic of democracy. Hans Küng elaborates on the participation of laity in Church leadership and elections in the first millennium where bishops were elected in some cases by acclamation of the people. Other theologians and scholars deal with examples of democratic experiments in the USA, Latin America, Brazil and the Netherlands. Charles Curran has a most interesting chapter on what Church governance systems can learn from official Catholic social teaching. His point is that we should practice in our church what we have been preaching to secular governments for over a century in regard to subsidiarity or decision making to be allowed to take place at the lowest possible level. Sister Marie Neal deals with the democratic process in the experience of American catholic women religious. Another scholar deals with the Protestant Experience and

Democratic Ecclesiology. The last chapter by the two editors gives a very useful historical overview and includes crucial comment on the lack of progress since Vatican II.

It is absolutely crucial for the Roman Catholic Church to develop beyond the monarchical structure if genuine reform is to be achieved. There is no need to reinvent the wheel. We can humbly learn from the state of the art practice as well as the mistakes of the broad Protestant experience since the Reformation. We can prepare to contribute our unique Catholic genius to the overall democratic governance systems and structures. It is up to us Catholic people by our voices, our letters, our walking away and withholding of funding to help to bring about the crucial and fundamental reform towards democratic and collegial systems.

12

COLLEGIALITY

Do not lord it over those entrusted to you, but be examples to the flock.

1 Peter 5, 3

The previous chapter discussed the fact that aspects of the democratic system correspond well with the dignity of all baptised persons and their active participation in the mission of Jesus Christ. The Catholic hierarchy has been strongly anti-modern for centuries and is no particular fan of democracy since the French Revolution. They are very uncomfortable with the idea that the collective wisdom of the people could be at variance with the pre-determined and infallible doctrines of the clerical magisterium. However, the more acceptable concept which predominates in official Church parlance is collegiality.

In the New Testament, we are told that Jesus sent out a group of disciples and apostles with the primacy or leadership of Peter.

Together, they had collective powers of healing and co-responsibility for spreading the Christian message and leading the way for local communities to experience the healing power and presence of the Risen Lord. Those communities would break bread together and have all things in common. They would receive the Holy Spirit and collaborate with chosen leaders by consensus in the mission of Jesus Christ.

Collegiality is the principle that the Church is a community (or college) of local churches which together make up the Church Universal. Each local church is overseen by a bishop who has fullness of orders and is preferably elected/selected by the People of God. Accordingly, the bishops are representatives of Christ and stewards of the mystery of God in their local community. They are elected for service and not domination. They are not mere branch managers of the local offices of the Holy See.

This fundamental Christian concept took on various forms during the course of history. It appears that the Church for part of the first millennium functioned in a somewhat collegial fashion. People seemed to have a vote in some cases and there were many great Councils or gatherings of leaders to resolve contentious matters of faith, doctrine or governance. Gradually, from the 4th century onwards, once Constantine installed Christianity as the official religion of the Roman Empire, the structures and systems of the Church became modelled on Roman imperial governance systems. Feudal systems entered the mix in later years and princes asserted their power in church matters. Tension began to emerge between Popes and the great Councils. From the Middle-Ages onwards, Rome seemed to predominate. This developed through the Council of Trent in 1545 as a response to the Reformation upheaval on towards Vatican Council I in 1869 which placed absolute emphasis on papal primacy and proclaimed the Pope as infallible. Papal primacy and central control by the Curia in Rome probably reached a high point in the early 20th century. A great debate developed at the Second Council in 1963 between bishops, pope and cardinals regarding collegiality and the precise relationship between papal primacy and the college of bishops. The bishops voted by a very large majority in September 1964 to approve *The Dogmatic Constitution on the Church* which appeared to restore more of a say to the College of Bishops. The final text appears in Chapter III of the Constitution. The text is seen as somewhat ambiguous and does not appear to finally resolve the tension between papal authority and the proper role of the College of Bishops. The huge change in governance and teaching which the bishops voted for in 1964 seemed to be a timely swing away from absolute papal power towards governance and teaching by the bishops of the entire worldwide church in union with the Pope. This appeared to be the correct historic reading of the signs of the times away from autocratic Roman Control towards the original collegial and counter-cultural governance of the Apostles with Peter.

This was a great move in theory but would require huge concessions by the minority bloc opposed to any updating or reform in Vatican II. They were never going to relinquish that dominant role which they had grabbed unjustly and to which they had become accustomed. Central monarchical control has the huge advantage of being the easiest to organise and enforce at least on the surface levels in the short term. Democratic or collegial systems are slow, complex, difficult and time-consuming. The great move in theory towards restoration of the rightful power of the College of Bishops would require new systems to incorporate the wisdom of the worldwide bishops in their collaboration with the Pope. Implementation of the rightful restoration of the role of the College of Bishops was always going to be the problem. The theory seemed to be that a Synod of Bishops representative of the Universal Church would be permanently in session and would be centrally involved in Church governance and teaching together with the Pope. This group of worldwide Bishops together with the Pope would be the rightful authority and would instruct the Curia in their much-reduced role as civil servants of the Pope working collegially with the Bishops. Such an independent and effective Synod of Bishops in permanent session has, tragically, never fully materialised as per the mandate of the huge majority of Bishops as Vatican II.

The first major victory for the Roman Control Group after the Council was their successful pressure on Pope Paul VI not to listen to or accept the *Report of the Birth Control Commission*. The collegial wisdom of the majority was dismissed and Pope Paul VI issued *Humanae Vitae* in 1968 with ongoing negative consequences within the Catholic Church. Pope John Paul II made it clear to bishops that their role was to obey him and not to countenance any kind of collegial governance as mandated by Vatican II. In the early 1980s, the Dutch Catholic Church whose episcopal conference made valiant attempts to consult the people and propose pastoral solutions for their country, got stopped in their tracks and completely neutralised by Rome. The Pope showed that he would not support any teaching role for the national conferences of bishops especially when they committed the folly of consulting lay people and priests. The overall tone of opposition to collegiality became clear during the pontificates of John Paul II and Benedict XVI. Pope John Paul II declared the issues of ordination of women as definitively settled and tried to cover this diktat with the cloak of infallibility. This was beyond his powers and utterly outrageous. Prayerful exploration of this hugely important topic had only just begun in recent decades within the Roman Catholic Church and it was utterly wrong to attempt to bully Catholic people into subservience.

The internal Roman coup against collegiality, co-responsibility, collaboration and consensus had quietly taken place in the decades since the Council. Sadly, the bishops were largely spineless and hamstrung in any efforts to right the wrong in the years up to 2013. Now, in the more hopeful pontificate of Pope Francis they seem unable to grasp the benign opportunity being offered to them to speak out and contribute their insights as to the pastoral needs of their people today. They seem reluctant or unable to retrieve the precious treasure of collegial wisdom of Bishops and Pope working together. Absolute loyalty to a Roman line on contraception, homosexuality, clerical authority and refusal to ordain women appears to have been one fundamental requirement towards being ordained bishop over the past few decades. Unfortunately, qualities of leadership, courage, empathy and active listening to the wisdom of the faithful may not have been a primary requirement. A bishop had to be anti-modern and totally obedient to the directives from central command even if that involved moving paedophiles to other parishes in order to protect the institution at all costs. The above coup had not escaped notice by many Catholic people worldwide. Understandably, many of them have exercised the option to walk away from this backward dynamic while retaining their deep faith in Jesus and the Christian ideal.

The book *Quo Vadis? Collegiality in the Code of Canon Law* by Mary McAleese, is a powerful study of this crucial topic and compares the theory with lack of progress towards implementation of the concept as voted for by the majority of bishops in Vatican II. Her book is a great contribution to the debate today as to "where are we going" or Quo Vadis? In her Author's Note she confirms that she is writing as one of Christ's faithful in accordance with Canon 212 of the 1983 Code of Canon Law. I include herewith the text of Item 3 within Canon 212:

> *According to the knowledge, competence and prestige which they possess, the Christian faithful have the right and even at times the duty to manifest to the sacred pastors their opinion on matters which pertain to the good of the Church and to make their opinion known to the rest of the Christian faithful, without*

prejudice to the integrity of faith or morals, with reverence towards their pastors, and attentive to common advantage and the dignity of persons.

We can all speak out and make our opinions known to the sacred pastors and the rest of the Christian faithful. In the light of the ongoing worldwide scandal in the Catholic Church, it is utterly crucial for lay people of honesty, courage and integrity to reclaim and renew the Catholic Church. Calling on the Holy Spirit, we have to work together in all kinds of groups to find effective and constructive ways to bring about reform in the Catholic Church and reunion of the Christian Churches.

13

JOIN THE PROTESTANTS – LEAVE THE CLUB

During our ongoing Catholic discussions, those of us Catholics who are raising questions are often told that we should go into exile and become refugees in some Protestant Church. This is the bitter voice which favours ongoing division whereas Jesus prayed that we should all be one. It seems more Christian and truthful to admit that all human institutions are fallible and have faults and that we all must consider the reforms that are needed. When there is no decent argument available to the institutional defenders in response to the issues that are troubling many ordinary Catholics, the last resort is to be told to go away. With eerie echoes of cruel Inquisition, we are ordered to leave the club and move away from loved ones in our religious family of origin. All we did was to raise questions about injustices. The threatening advice to leave the club sounds suspiciously like the merciless practice in the previous century to force single pregnant women out of the family and into an institution. The old instructions to attack the whistle-blower rather than the problem comes into operation. The theses of the original reformers were all dismissed, and the result was war, destruction and division over the past centuries. The scandal of disunity among Christians is one of the greatest obstacles to evangelisation today. The diagnosis by Pope John XXIII in the early 1960s that updating and reunion is the answer, remains valid. Instead of splitting and sundering, all Christian Churches need to work together towards cooperation and reunion.

Catholics who were programmed not to question and who order reformers to leave the Catholic tribe may be operating from the following outdated catechisms, instructions and mindsets:

19th CENTURY/VATICAN I CATECHISM

Some Catholics resisted and continue to resist the teaching of Vatican II as formulated by very large majorities of the bishops. Those people have asserted that the modern world is suspect and that there can be no advance on clerical teaching beyond the early 20th century. There has been much change in all facets of life since the time of the Penny Catechism and the infallible claims of Vatican I. It is easy to see the problems in communication when some Catholics are operating out of a Vatican I mentality and many others have progressed to a Vatican II understanding of the Catholic religion. Most of us have moved on from the pay/pray/obey role assigned to lay people in an earlier world of clericalism. Most of us have moved on from the arrogant assertion of salvation only within the Roman Catholic Church. Most of us have moved on from contempt for reformers towards ecumenical respect for all Protestants and all religions. We have come to accept that the process of change, development, exodus and evolution moves ahead in the whole world as a natural law. Vatican II encouraged us to pray the New Testament and meet Jesus with his radical options of love for all and inclusion of the marginalised. We noted that the Pharisees and their hate groups constantly confronted him with their outdated traditions and narrow legalism.

INQUISITION MINDSET

Unfortunately, some institutions and powerful individuals cannot tolerate any criticism or admit wrongdoing. A free press and media is unwelcome. We are all horrified by the tragic results for reformers, dissenters and journalists. We want no more secrecy or Inquisition-type courts. We reject censorship, the silencing of priests and the banning of books. We favour due process and complete transparency. We, Catholic people, do not want to go into exile from the faith community into which we were born. We experienced much love there and a preponderance of good people untainted by power. While we have become aware of serious injustices within an outdated institution, we treasure the eternal truths which give us meaning and purpose. We would prefer to stay in and work for reform and reunion. We reserve the right to use our critical faculties. We are not trying to start a new religion – there are plenty of religions.

ROMAN EMPIRE MINDSET

That empire collapsed centuries ago. Unfortunately, rotten vestiges of imperial structures and attitudes poison the institution of the Catholic Church to this day. Today, most Catholics are proud democrats and value healthy debate, dissent and dialogue leading to consensus and change. We do not like dictatorship under any holy vestments and are very uncomfortable with a religious monarchy. We want to move on from imperial times, systems and structures. We want the concept of collegiality from Vatican II to be put into practice for all Catholics. We think it is healthy and wholesome for all to speak out, listen and dialogue.

COVER-UP/DEFLECT/SMOKESCREEN/RED HERRING TACTICS

When Catholic persons cannot admit the obvious problems of injustice and outdated practices in an unreformed institution and the clerical system must be defended at all costs, you may hear some of the following comments viz;

- *"Sure, I am happy with old ways and everything is grand."*
- *"You are whinging and anti-Catholic."*
- *"You are angry and polemical and over the top."*
- *"You are a maverick or a heretic."*
- *"You are disgusting and there is nothing to see here."*
- *"You are a disobedient priest or lay person."*
- *"No, you were never abused. You only want to bash the Church and grab money."*
- *"I reserve my right as a cleric to have mental reservations in anything I say."*
- *"It would be an appalling vista to admit that reformers and prophets might have been right centuries ago."*
- *"She has an agenda."*

PARANOIA/FALSE VICTIM MODE

Some bishops adopt an utterly false victim mode and talk of hostility towards or persecution of the Church. It all depends on whether you define the Church as hierarchy or the People of God. I do not think that there is widespread hostility towards the People of God who continue to go about full of love and doing massive good. Many Catholics advance beyond childish deference and have serious disagreement with some clerical teachings on the lower levels of religious beliefs. It is a total untruth to label that disagreement with clerics on minor issues as hostility or persecution of the People of God.

PART 3

CALL TO ACTION

BE THE CHANGE

14

NEW WORDS – NEW NARRATIVE – NEW ACTION

There are many doctrines which no longer make sense to the modern mind. Those doctrines need to be reviewed and reformulated if they contain value. The Old Testament writings in various genres and styles were assembled from the oral traditions of Middle Eastern communities three thousand years ago. The New Testament is itself a new narrative or evolution of the story. The core religious truth does not change, namely, that reality is gracious rather than absurd and meaningless. Even within the New Testament, there are different emphases and narratives depending on the needs of various writers and communities. Today, two thousand years later, much has happened and there are different levels of religious experience, knowledge, insight, science and understanding of Creation and ourselves. Accordingly, many doctrines, theological theories and formulations from the Old Testament and first millennium are out of date today and serve to turn people away from Jesus Christ. I found it jarring to hear talk about indulgences from the Vatican in connection with Pope Francis' visit to Ireland in 2018. I thought that we had moved beyond all of that. The corruption around that same topic in the Middle Ages contributed to the Reformation breakup. This topic is an example of where there should be deletion and removal or else a totally new narrative. Limbo was a part of the story given to us in the Penny Catechism. It was a burden for mothers where there was miscarriage or death before baptism. Now that item has been removed from that narrative. Many doctrines and teachings such as Heaven, Hell and Purgatory need to be explained in modern concepts or language. St Paul taught in Ephesians (6:5) "slaves, obey your earthly masters with fear and trembling." That is still in the New Testament. It took too many centuries for us to move from that Pauline doctrine on slavery to a new narrative that slavery and true Christianity are incompatible.

I find some Old Testament readings to be strange and difficult or out of sync with today. There are very few Scripture scholars available in our parishes to interpret those readings. Some of the homilies may only add to the confusion especially in the current situation where there is no opportunity for robust debate or challenge. An example of new narrative or wording is resurrection of the dead in the Nicene Creed while the Apostles Creed refers to resurrection of the body. The different wording could have some relevance within the changed Catholic teaching about cremation. Over the centuries, various Councils, Catechisms and encyclicals have advanced new formulations of doctrine. Vatican II was a long overdue attempt to produce an updated narrative.

Popes, bishops, priests and religious have the ongoing opportunity to form the narrative. Various mystics, poets, scientists, thinkers and ordinary people strive to make their contribution. Sometimes, that is in the face of official Church opposition and without the benefit of a pulpit. Father Teilhard de Chardin S.J. (1881-1955) was a priest and palaeontologist whom I studied during the course of my science degree. His writings did not find favour in Rome. He strove to combine the best of his scientific knowledge with his mystical religious vision of the cosmic Christ. He wrote about the phenomenon of man and the divine milieu. He attempted to build up a new narrative that would reconcile Christian theology with the scientific theory of evolution.

Other writers who are exploring new narratives for the 21st century are listed in the bibliography. These include, Matthew Fox, Michael Morwood, Fr Diarmuid O'Murchu, Ilia Delio, Brian Swimme and Thomas Berry. In recent decades, we had the late John Moriarty as mystic, poet and Kerry storyteller. Pope Francis with *Laudato Si* and writers such as Fr Sean McDonagh are trying to alert us to the emerging narrative in regard to climate change and the serious challenges arising from that potential catastrophe.

I struggle with the following questions about certain doctrines. I suspect many Catholics have similar questions:

IS GOD MALE?

Is the Trinity all male persons? Is God only Abba Father? As human beings, we struggle to describe or name God. Pope John Paul I is quoted as saying, "God is father, but ever more God is mother." Is our traditional and valuable devotion to Our Lady a wink and nod in the direction of the female dimension of God? There are two very interesting books on this topic by an American theologian named

Elizabeth Johnson - *She Who Is* and *Quest for the Living God: Mapping Frontiers in the Theology of God.*

OLD TESTAMENT

Genesis and other Old Testament books raise many questions. Is God an angry patriarch in the skies? Are we stained from conception and marked with some original sin committed by Eve and Adam? Are we born flawed in the depths of our sexuality and humanity? I read in chapter 2 of Genesis about God creating man and placing him in a Garden of Eden full of delicious and enticing trees. Yet, this God forbade access to the seemingly important Tree of Knowledge of good and evil. I wonder if this a capricious God toying with us and restricting freedom? Chapter 3 of Genesis deals with the serpent tempting Eve to disobey God and encouraging her to eat the good fruit from the Tree of Knowledge. Is this text anti-woman? Is Eve portrayed as a disobedient temptress and easily fooled by a snake? Is this story about ancient sexual anxiety and pessimism? Did the myth or story emerge to explain death? We have a different perspective on Creation and Evolution today. Did sin and death come in to the world because of one woman or man? Does an angry God demand sacrifice and martyrdom from Jesus or any Son of Man? Was there too much emphasis on blood sacrifice, cruelty and crucifixion? Should some of the Old Testament stories be left in the past and should we advance with New Testament insights in order to encounter God's Word and Revelation today? Are Jews the only Chosen People and all others to be destroyed by the armies of God?

SEXUALITY

I think that all narrative and doctrine around the very important topic of sexuality needs to be reviewed and reformulated by mature women and men. Such Catholics with wholesome experience and broad education will strive to articulate the complex dimensions of our sacred sexuality as we celebrate enhanced life and mutual support as well as joyful generation of new life. Clerical teaching in the official Catholic Catechism states that every sexual thought, word, desire and action outside of marriage is a mortal sin in every instance. Sexual acts within marriage that are not open to conception are also viewed as mortal sins. I think that it is utterly wrong for an elite group of men with no proper training, expertise or experience to place the above burden of guilt, fear or scrupulosity on people today. It is good to see that Catholic people in recent decades are shaking off that oppression. Yet, within our rituals and Masses there is mention of Mary not losing the glory of her virginity, Immaculate Conception and Virgin Birth. Understandably, many Catholics find all this narrative at odds with a positive and healthy celebration of sexuality.

Old Testament texts concerning homosexuality continue to divide and bother people in various Churches. Traditionalists seem to be imprisoned in an unchanging world and a literal interpretation of some Old Testament stories while disregarding lots of other instructions and practices. Jesus says nothing about homosexuality but concentrates on love, service and inclusion. He got into trouble with the Pharisees because of his association with the marginalised. However, the official 1994 *Catechism of the Catholic Church* talks of homosexual acts as "grave depravity, intrinsically disordered and contrary to natural law." The Catechism also talks of the "homosexual condition as a trial." The writers of the Catechism do not appear to have learned anything from modern medicine or psychiatry, experience of homosexual persons or the theological understanding that all of God's creation, whether heterosexual or homosexual, is indeed good. What counts is the loving actions of all persons to build relationships, marriages and families.

Where love is, there God is, and, accordingly, all will be well. I have listened to the stories of homosexual friends and the new insights emerging over the past fifty years regarding sexuality. I have moved away from the unchanging clerical teaching on homosexual actions as intrinsically disordered. While the majority of people are heterosexual, God's creation includes a valuable complementary minority of homosexual persons. I do not accept that their actions are intrinsically disordered as stated by the *Catechism of the Catholic Church* and the clerics and groups locked into absolute loyal obedience to that unchanging dogmatic line. They are different, equal, valuable and good.

I am proud to have voted yes with the majority of Irish voters on 22 May 2015 for marriage equality. Love, marriage, commitment and family is very important. I am delighted that Irish Catholic people said no to homophobia and yes to the power of love, inclusion and marriage equality. While we still hear the horror stories of homophobic bullying and violence, most of us today are glad to be part of modern societies that have advanced to a position of love, respect and justice for all LGBT+ persons. It is right for us to challenge Catholic doctrine on this important issue and assert firmly that we do not wish to collude with or contribute to the harassment, abuse or denigration of LGBT+ persons. The bishops state that "marriage is a total communion of life and love with God of the married couple in their family life." If you have come to an awareness that homosexual persons are not intrinsically disordered but are a different/equal/blessed/complementary part of God's wonderful creation, then you will respect their love for each other and the presence of God where love is and their equal ability to marry, form a family and parent inspired by the Holy Spirit of Love.

SACRAMENT OF PENANCE

Most Catholics in Ireland have walked away from the frequent Confession of earlier times. Simultaneously, many people appreciate the need to talk in confidence and the value of a good listener. Some Catholics had bad experiences in confession with priests of stunted development and warped thinking to do with sex and women. Scrupulosity enslaved some people. Stories emerged of abusers pardoning abusers and concealment of crimes from Gardaí under orders from some spiritual superior. The above factors and other societal developments have affected our use of the Sacrament of Penance. I am aware of the great response in the few parishes which today offer some format of General Absolution as part of the sacramental encounter. If there remains some healing value in the reformed celebration of the Sacrament of Penance, and I think there does, then we need to construct a new presentation and structure for this encounter with a merciful God and new beginnings in our life. The official Roman Catholic Institution needs to give the good example of confession and repentance.

PAPAL INFALLIBILITY
The idea that a human being or a human institution cannot err is unbelievable today. Claims to infallibility were rushed through in 1870 for dubious reasons. It is not at all clear how such a claim tallies with the early Church or the realities of today. Many papal and Church proclamations have changed over the course of history. Papal infallibility is a major obstacle to reunion. This particular element of the overall narrative needs to be reviewed.

Clearly there is much narrative and doctrine for the Catholic community to discuss and speak out about. It is easy and tempting to teach simple old stories to innocent children in our Catholic schools. It is far more challenging and difficult to deal with the questions which arise from Catholic adults. The adults will only be evangelised if the Jesus story and narrative makes sense to them in the modern world. They, in turn, will be the best teachers and exemplars for their children.

15

FUTURE PARISH – FUTURE PRIEST

For many are called, but few are chosen.   Matthew 21, 14

If the key elements in the current Catholic crisis have not been tackled, I do not see a great surge from the next generations to replace us in the parishes or churches. If the reforms as highlighted in this book have not happened, many parishes will wither and die. I think that will be a loss. Parish and local community is very important in different dimensions of our life together. Loss of parish will make the world a poorer place since I am convinced that prayer, worship and encounter with a vibrant local community is important for us all. Jesus invited us to gather in groups in order to share a meal in memory of Him. He promised a Holy Spirit of new life, love and care for the whole community. The Christian message centres on the importance of community, caring for others and action for justice. It is the opposite of selfish individualism and greedy concentration on our isolated self-interest. Inspiration obtained from your local

Catholic parish can spur people to active involvement in other groups for the common good.

The future parish will be based on shared leadership and decision-making. People and priests need to assess their real felt needs and produce action plans. There must be open communication with the bishop and advocacy for Vatican III. There must be a renewed emphasis on ecumenical co-operation and lessons can be learned from the reformed churches. *Great Catholic Parishes* by William E Simon Jr., is an American publication about how some parishes are successfully nurturing their spiritual families. Four key sections state the following: great parishes share leadership, great parishes foster spiritual maturity and plan for discipleship, great parishes excel on Sunday and great parishes evangelise. *Tomorrow's Parish* by Donal Harrington is a similar discussion of faith communities and parishes in the Irish context.

Laity have no direct participation in the appointment, supervision or removal of any priest or bishop. Priests retain total control and parish councils, even when tolerated, are purely consultative. I fear that outdated model of parish will not win many people tomorrow. The future parish needs to be organised into small basic Christian communities with trained leaders. This model has worked well in Latin America and other regions. I would suggest organising parishes into zones with small outreach teams to visit, communicate and assess pastoral needs. I know this is all very utopian and would require the approval and positive cooperation of Catholic people. The future parish should involve outreach to the adults who are the ones to be converted and evangelised. However, that won't happen if adults are unhappy in an unreformed clerical set up. If the adults are won back to personal prayer in the home and church attendance post-Vatican III, then they will model for the children and carry forward the basic good work done in the schools. Presuming that the active participation together with financial support of the parish is restored again to the required levels, then parishes can provide many varied new ministries to meet current needs.

Reports indicate that morale is low for some priests and that they are operating under too much stress and pressure. Some suffer from loneliness, isolation and mental health issues. Priests see a system slowly dying and it is very difficult for them to talk honestly about it. They have fears about their own priestly identity and some are afraid to engage even with fellow clergy. There are too many demands on priests and very little backup care and support. The priest is often the first port of call in time of crisis, tragedy and suicide. The priests are suffering for the sins of a few and the cover-up by superiors. We should help the priests in any way we can, conscious that they are operating within the rules of a different system. All of them are doing their best within a problematic culture of clericalism. Reports from priests' conferences reveal that there is much room for improvement in the relationships between bishops and priests. All rights of priests should be respected. Bishops should treat them properly as equal professional colleagues. Priests will be more content and more likely to provide good pastoral care if they are treated fairly by the bishops. One way we can assist priests is to use our freedom to speak out clearly to bishops and Nuncio for massive reform in the Catholic Church.

It seems to me that the era of the priest as a male superior caste is drawing towards a close. The era of equality between ordained priesthood and baptised priesthood of lay people needs to emerge in the ministry, governance and teaching of the Church. There is a multitude of charisms, gifts and ministries to be recognised and utilised. All can contribute according to their talent and the burden is shared. Future priest can be woman or man, married or single. The future priest should be a healthy and mature disciple of Jesus Christ full of faith, hope, love and laughter. She or he should have good self-esteem and solid empathy. He or she should be a prayerful servant leader able to encounter and celebrate God in all of creation. She or he should be comfortable in sharing leadership and be a good co-ordinator of multiple ministries.

I know the good that can accrue for individuals and the parish community if there is a happy, healthy, Christlike priest doing good and enlivening people. The pastoral priest listens to the people and strives to bridge the gap between the official clerical line and painful human realities. The priest can be an inspirer, animator, spiritual guide and moderator. Where the priest is enthusiastic, this will transmit to the parish community. Working closely with all parishioners, a wholesome, mature priest can provide leadership and facilitate the joint ministry of various talented persons.

Bishops, priests and people have a challenge ahead if we are to say "no" to clericalism and move towards new types of parishes, faith communities and ministries. We can learn from other Christian Churches. Then we should move forward and set free our Catholic genius, creativity and goodness to devise those new forms of ministry and parish.

16

PLAN OF ACTION – TOGETHER WE CAN

Follow the Leader

I have listened to people and I have spoken out. I have written letters to the papers and been active in reform groups for decades. I have been active in my parish and plan to continue to volunteer as long as I am able. I have compiled this book and am prepared to join in a follow-up conversation with any interested group. In response to Pope Francis who has asked for our opinions, I have written to my bishop, pastoral area priests and the Papal Nuncio. Copies of those letters are at the end of this book. But, what is needed now is people power. Your letters, action and contribution in parish assemblies are absolutely crucial.

The bishops, priests and Nuncios need to receive a large and very broad sample of the opinions of Catholic people. In the absence of widespread parish assemblies and open diocesan synods, letters from Catholics may be one small, practical way for them to obtain a sense of Catholic faith and wisdom. This will surely help them in their decision-making as we move towards Vatican III. We take it that the bishops, priests and Nuncios are not like the unjust judge in the gospel story who will continue to disregard us from within a world of clericalism. We act on the assumption that those men are sincere pastoral priests open to the Spirit speaking forth from all the baptised.

A just, collegial and compassionate Catholic Church which has clearly abandoned misogyny and clericalism will be a more wholesome community and in a better position to sustain and be a force for good in the world. Together, we can speak out our opinions and inform our sacred pastors in regard to the good sense of the People of God. Together, we can contribute to a new Catholic conversation and prepare the way for Vatican III. Together, we can provide momentum towards reform, renewal and reunion. Now, it is over to us.

FIVE AIMS FOR REFORM

The following five issues are of serious concern for me.

1. EQUALITY/DEMOCRACY/POWERSHARING/COLLEGIALITY

There must be equality and active participation for all baptised Catholics in the mission of Christ to build up the Kingdom of God. Clericalism must be phased out. The priesthood of all Catholics is important and must be developed in accordance with personal charism and the needs of the community. There must be power-sharing and a role for all in decision-making. Collegial and democratic structures must be urgently developed under Canon Law. All should have a voice and a real say in the appointment of servant leaders. There must be open and honest communication leading to consensus and change. Bishops must listen to people and priests. In this way, they can discern the good sense of Catholics as they make urgent preparation for Vatican III. Bishops will then be in a better position to assess the pastoral needs of their region and should assert their full collegial role with the Pope as envisaged in Vatican II.

2. EQUALITY/ORDINATION FOR WOMEN

There must be equality for women and full participation by them in the reformed ministry, governance and teaching office of the Catholic Church. There must be ordination of women as a matter of justice. We need the talents of all to build up our local parishes. Apartheid for women must end now. The Catholic Church should provide moral leadership instead of cover for primitive groups who persist in discrimination against women. Other Christian churches and secular society have provided moral leadership. Best practice in Catholic families centres on love, respect and power sharing for women. It is not possible to evangelise today in the language of patriarchy, sexism and misogyny. We, Catholic people, do not wish to collude any longer in the abuse, harassment or denigration of women.

3. PRIMACY OF CONSCIENCE

There has been renewed emphasis on the primacy of conscience and religious liberty since Vatican II. Development of a fully informed conscience and moral action based thereon is of benefit to society. The faithful give careful consideration to clerical teaching as well as the common sense of the People of God and a broad spectrum of information. Most Catholic couples do not accept or assent to the clerical teaching on contraception. After due consideration, most Catholics have given primacy to their conscience on this matter as well as issues such as homosexuality and divorce. The clerical teaching on sexual issues needs to be reviewed and discussed by the Catholic People of God if we are an honest and wholesome

134

community. Parish practice in regard to the important Sacrament of Penance needs to be discussed, reviewed and reformed.

4. POSITIVE/RESPONSIBLE SEXUALITY

Positive and responsible celebration of our sexuality is crucial for all and must now be promoted. Many Biblical and liturgical texts are based on an outdated worldview which is unfair to women. Any narrative within our church which denigrates healthy sexuality or texts which extol virginity over marriage needs to be discussed and reviewed. Catholic people prize the ideal of faithful marriage for life but accept the reality that some marriages break down. Such persons should not be denied Eucharist or parish welcome and support. Enforced celibacy for priests is an abuse and injustice which should end now. It has contributed to church break up in the past. It is a factor in sexually deviant behaviour. Today it contributes to a Eucharistic and pastoral care famine. Old Testament homophobia needs to be re-examined and changed just like teaching on usury, slavery and anti-Semitism.

5. INCLUSIVE CHURCH/CHURCH UNITY

We must promote an inclusive Church which is open and welcoming to all. Our Church should not marginalise people because of sexual orientation, marital situation or for any other reason. All are welcome to the table of the Lord. Our presentation as a Catholic Church should bring good news of a loving God represented by Good Samaritan people feeding the hungry and working for justice with the disadvantaged, oppressed or marginalised. Disunity among Christians is an ongoing scandal and a major obstacle to evangelisation. We must provide greater ecumenical leadership as well as a renewed emphasis on co-operation and eventual reunion in diversity.

PLAN OF ACTION

Write/Email/Talk

Pope Francis has asked for our opinions. Write or email your opinions and suggestions for reform to your bishop, priest and Papal Nuncio. Addresses are given in Appendix B at the end of the book. Write to your parish council and newspapers. Talk to friends and neighbours. Speak out in parish assemblies or on media. Become a member of *We Are Church Ireland* and contribute your ideas to the site or Facebook page.

Start a Small Group

Gather two or three or more in your home with similar concerns about the Catholic Church – even if only for a limited twelve-month experiment. It can be a discussion group, a prayer group, a bible study group or a book club. Small basic communities are probably going to be an important part of future Catholic worship and prayer. Sell this book and promote this project in your parish. Operate as a small group to lobby your priest and parish council. You have been empowered through baptism and have your own unique talents. Discuss the crisis and the real pastoral needs of your area. Help out where at all possible in your local parish.

Silent Protest and Message

When addressed from the pulpit about vocations, shortage of priests or parish clustering, raise your hand for a short while in silent protest and to signal your awareness of the charade of praying for vocations subject to medieval clerical restrictions. Show your anger at the needless and self-inflicted Eucharistic and pastoral care famine. Your protest will hopefully deliver the message that a man-made celibacy law and a tradition which excludes women is outdated and can be changed. Declare that you value priesthood and Eucharistic celebration but require an end to clericalism and the abuse which has arisen from a disordered meaning system. Point out that God is indeed providing persons in every parish with the talent and vocation for service, reformed priesthood and renewed parish ministry. Blow the whistle on the episcopal policy of bringing in priests from the developing world without parish consultation and under the suspicion that the practice is a delaying tactic to avoid tackling root problems. Encourage the bishops to listen to their priests and to support them. Inform the bishops that Catholics want reformed ministry, structures and systems.

Finance

It seems right to contribute to your parish in some way as long as you continue to practice there. Request a clear, transparent and regular account from the parish priest in regard to all assets, income and expenditure. Explain that your contribution is at a minimum level until there is serious reform in the Church but that you are glad to continue maximum support for various Catholic charities.

PART 4

SPEAK OUT

LETTERS

17

SPEAK OUT – LETTER TO BISHOP

Archbishop Diarmuid Martin,
Archbishop's House,
Drumcondra,
Dublin 9

14 November 2018

Re: Response to the invitation from Pope Francis to speak out our opinions

Dear Bishop Martin,

I am a practising Catholic in this diocese. I have been active in my local parish of St Attracta's, Meadowbrook and in various Catholic reform groups. I retain faith in the core Good News of Jesus Christ but disagree with clerical teaching on contraception, enforced celibacy, suppression of women and homophobia. I know you are concerned about the Catholic crisis and alienation. I agree with you that the unjust treatment of women in the Catholic Church is the main problem. I welcome your recent letter to priests encouraging parish assemblies to discuss the future. This process should be of benefit as long as real issues are discussed and significant change is allowed to proceed. If the assemblies prove to be only pious talking shops smothered by clerical roadblocks to change, then the exercise may tick some boxes but will only breed deeper cynicism.

Pope Francis has repeatedly asked us to speak out our opinions about the changes that are needed at this time of crisis in the Catholic Church. I am responding to him by writing to yourself as well as my parish priest and the Papal Nuncio. I am inviting other Catholics to do the same. I also welcomed the historic Letter of Pope Francis to the People of God (20 August 2018). He proclaimed that we must say an emphatic "no" to all forms of clericalism and that Catholics should drive forward for massive reform. I presume this means women and men sharing in service, ordained ministry, leadership and governance.

Practising Catholics are concerned that many adult colleagues and most young people have become alienated from Sunday mass and parish involvement. In my opinion, the following factors are among the reasons for Catholic alienation. Bad news about abuses arising from disordered clericalism is pervasive and obscures excellent Catholic services ongoing in homes, parishes and areas of social need. Lay Catholics do not wish to collude with the abuse of children, women, priests or power. Most Catholics have not accepted the clerical teaching on birth control. Catholics value democracy and power-sharing and disapprove of medieval structures of government in the Church. Polls show that a majority of Irish Catholics favour women priests and married priests. They resent the charade of praying for restricted vocations and sense that there are good people in every parish with the vocation for service, ministry and leadership. Catholics are alarmed at the self-inflicted Eucharistic and pastoral care famine and are concerned about overburdened priests. The episcopal policy of bringing in priests from the developing world without consulting the faithful, may help in the short term but only represents cynical retention of clericalism and refusal to ordain married women and men. Catholic people prize the ideal of faithful marriage for life but accept the reality that some marriages break down. We agree with Pope Francis that such persons should not be denied Eucharist or parish welcome and support. A majority of Irish Catholics reject homophobia and respect LGBT+ persons. Government reports, such as Murphy, Ryan, etc. have sickened people and they have walked away. Adding to the distress, the Roman control brigade appears deaf and irreformable and living in a different world. Accordingly, moving away from clericalism and doing good elsewhere in God's presence is one sensible option for free persons. They are unlikely to return without evidence of significant progress. While such persons remain disillusioned and alienated from Catholicism, they are unlikely to enhance the religious instruction provided to their children in school.

I disagree with the suggestion that the Catholic Church should become smaller and reserved only for a conservative elite as a truly anti-modern group. I think the Gospel is for all people. The Catholic religion needs to be presented in new narrative, modern language and concepts, renewed ritual as well as updated structures. It is not possible to evangelise people today in the language of sexism, misogyny, patriarchy, monarchy, homophobia and exclusion. Elements of that language in the Catholic presentation are a hindrance to parents trying to transmit the faith.

There has been a lack of conversation, dialogue and honest communication among us Catholics. All aspects of worship, ritual and liturgical celebration require urgent review, improvement and updating. Massive reform of ministry, leadership and governance together with parish renewal is sorely needed. There must be greater emphasis on ecumenical cooperation to facilitate enriched faith encounter with Jesus Christ. A deficient and one-sided Church institution cannot convey joyful news of life to the full. A just, collegial and compassionate Church clearly working with the marginalised for justice and improved conditions will prove to be a beacon of hope.

Bishops should listen to priests and people via assemblies and synods in preparation for Vatican III. I trust that bishops will cooperate with Pope Francis from February 2019 onwards to implement a far-reaching plan of action against abuse and clericalism. Thank you for your kind attention to my concerns. I also enclose a copy of my Five Aims for Reform. May the Lord bless you in your life and ministry.

I am,

Yours faithfully,

_____

Joe Mulvaney

cc. Archbishop Eamon Martin, Ara Coeli, Armagh, Northern Ireland BT61 7QY
cc. The Secretary, Irish Catholic Bishops Conference, Columba Centre, Maynooth, Co Kildare
cc. Bishop Raymond Field, 3 Castleknock Road, Blanchardstown, Dublin 15
cc. Bishop Eamonn Walsh, Naomh Brid, Blessington Road, Tallaght, Dublin 24

Enc 1

18

SPEAK OUT – LETTER TO PARISH PRIEST

14 November 2018

Re: Response to the invitation from Pope Francis to speak out our opinions

Dear Father

Normally, we meet and chat at busy parish council meetings. We have not had any opportunity for serious personal conversation or dialogue. However, at this time of bad news and crisis in the Catholic Church, I am writing to you to outline some of my opinions and suggestions. I retain faith in the core Good News of Jesus Christ but disagree with clerical teaching on contraception, enforced celibacy, suppression of women and homophobia. Pope Francis has repeatedly asked us to speak out our opinions about the reforms that are needed at this time in the Catholic Church. I am responding to him by writing to yourself as well as my bishop and the Papal Nuncio. I am inviting other Catholics to do the same. I also welcomed the historic Letter of Pope Francis to the People of God (20 August 2018). He proclaimed that we must say an emphatic "no" to all forms of clericalism and that Catholics should drive forward for massive reform. I presume this means women and men sharing in service, ordained ministry, leadership and governance.

I have been an active member of St Attracta's parish since 1978. This is a great faith community and I want it to grow. Despite part-time help from two Nigerian priests, it is increasingly difficult for yourself and one other priest to provide comprehensive pastoral care over three large parishes. Pastoral councils with empowered lay leadership must be freed of clerical control and organise to meet the real needs of the parish. I welcome the advocacy of Archbishop Martin for parish assemblies. This process should be of benefit as long as real issues are discussed and significant reform is allowed to proceed. If the assemblies prove to be only pious talking shops smothered by clerical roadblocks to change, then the exercise may tick some boxes but will only breed deeper cynicism.

Practising Catholics are concerned that many adult colleagues and most young people have become alienated from Sunday mass and parish involvement. In my opinion, the following factors are among the reasons for Catholic alienation. Bad news about abuses arising from disordered clericalism is pervasive and obscures excellent Catholic services ongoing in homes, parishes and areas of social need. Lay Catholics do not wish to collude with the abuse of children, women, priests or power. Most Catholics have not accepted the clerical teaching on birth control. Catholics value democracy and power-sharing and disapprove of medieval structures of government in the Church. Polls show that a majority of Irish Catholics favour women priests and married priests. They resent the charade of praying for restricted vocations and sense that there are good people in every parish with the vocation for service, ministry and leadership. Catholics are alarmed at the self-inflicted Eucharistic and pastoral care famine and are concerned about overburdened priests. The episcopal policy of bringing in priests from the developing world without consulting the faithful, may help in the short term but only represents cynical retention of clericalism and refusal to ordain married women and men. Catholic people prize the ideal of faithful marriage for life but accept the reality that some marriages break down. We agree with Pope Francis that such persons should not be denied Eucharist or parish welcome and support. A majority of Irish Catholics reject homophobia and respect LGBT+ persons. Government reports, such as Murphy, Ryan, etc. have sickened people and they have walked away. Adding to the distress, the Roman control brigade appears deaf and irreformable and living in a different world. Accordingly, moving away from clericalism and doing good elsewhere in God's presence is one sensible option for free persons. They are unlikely to return without evidence of significant progress. While such persons remain disillusioned and alienated from Catholicism, they are unlikely to enhance the religious instruction provided to their children in school.

I disagree with the suggestion that the Catholic Church should become smaller and reserved only for a conservative elite as a truly anti-modern group. I think the Gospel is for all people. The Catholic religion needs to be presented in new narrative, modern language and concepts, renewed ritual as well as updated structures. It is not possible to evangelise people today in the language of sexism, misogyny, patriarchy, monarchy, homophobia and exclusion. Elements of that language in the Catholic presentation are a hindrance to parents trying to transmit the faith.

There has been a lack of conversation, dialogue and honest communication among us Catholics. All aspects of worship, ritual and liturgical celebration require urgent review, improvement and updating. Massive reform of ministry, leadership and governance together with parish renewal is sorely needed. There must be greater emphasis on ecumenical cooperation to facilitate enriched faith encounter with Jesus Christ. A deficient and one-sided Church institution cannot convey joyful news of life to the full. A just, collegial and compassionate Church clearly working with the marginalised for justice and improved conditions will prove to be a beacon of hope.

I also enclose a copy of my Five Aims for Reform. I appreciate that priests have promised obedience to bishops. However, I hope that you and other pastoral priests will have the courage to challenge the prevailing clerical culture and help us all on the road to reform. Thank you for your kind attention to my concerns and for your service and ministry among us.

I am,

Yours faithfully,

_____

Joe Mulvaney

Cc: pastoral area priests and deacons

Enc 1

19

SPEAK OUT – LETTER TO PAPAL NUNCIO

Archbishop Jude Thaddeus Okolo
The Apostolic Nunciature
183 Navan Road
Dublin 7

14 November 2018

Re: Response to the invitation from Pope Francis to speak out our opinions

Dear Bishop Okolo,

I am delighted to welcome you as the first African person to be appointed Papal Nuncio to Ireland. I know that you are much-travelled and that you have rich experience in the diplomatic service. I trust that you have encountered great Irish missionaries and volunteers providing service to your home continent. We, too, are blessed in our Irish parishes with excellent priests from your home country Nigeria.

I am a practising Catholic deeply influenced by Pope John XXIII and Vatican II. I like the idea of "opening up the windows" and updating as an ongoing strategy if we are to have any hope as parents to pass on the faith. I am involved in my parish and in various Catholic reform groups. I retain faith in the core Good News of Jesus Christ but disagree with clerical teaching on contraception, enforced celibacy, suppression of women and homophobia.

Pope Francis has repeatedly asked us to speak out our opinions about the reforms that are needed at this time of crisis in the Catholic Church. I am responding to him by writing to yourself as well as my parish priest and bishop. I am inviting other Catholics to do the same. I also welcomed the historic Letter of Pope Francis to the People of God (20 August 2018). He proclaimed that we must say an emphatic "no" to all forms of clericalism and that Catholics should drive forward for massive reform. I presume this means women and men sharing in service, ordained ministry, leadership and governance.

While we are enduring some serious crises here in Ireland, much development has taken place in this republic over the past century. Irish people have a resistance to monarchy or imperial domination by external rulers. Catholic Church hierarchy wielded too much control in the past but that has now changed. A majority of Irish people are Catholic but do not accept all clerical teachings. Irish Catholics have been horrified by clerical abuse and official cover-up. There is no evidence yet that Rome has undertaken a major review of the meaning system and clerical culture which produces abuse. We were shocked that Marie Collins – an Irish woman survivor – felt forced to resign in 2017 from a Roman Commission dealing with child safety. She encountered clerical resistance to best practice. Irish people were also scandalised in recent decades at harsh treatment meted out by Roman officials to Irish priests and theologians who dared to raise valid questions.

Practising Catholics are concerned that many adult colleagues and most young people have become alienated from Sunday mass and parish involvement. In my opinion, the following factors are among the reasons for Catholic alienation. Bad news about abuses arising from disordered clericalism is pervasive and obscures excellent Catholic services ongoing in homes, parishes and areas of social need. Lay Catholics do not wish to collude with the abuse of children, women, priests or power. Most Catholics have not accepted the clerical teaching on birth control. Catholics value democracy and power-sharing and disapprove of medieval structures of government in the Church. Polls show that a majority of Irish Catholics favour women priests and married priests. They resent the charade of praying for restricted vocations and sense that there are good people in every parish with the vocation for service, ministry and leadership. Catholics are alarmed at the self-inflicted Eucharistic and pastoral care famine and are concerned about overburdened priests. The episcopal policy of bringing in priests from the developing world without consulting the faithful, may help in the short term but only represents cynical retention of clericalism and refusal to ordain married women and men. Catholic people prize the ideal of faithful marriage for life but accept the reality that some marriages break down. We agree with Pope Francis that such persons should not be denied Eucharist or parish welcome and support. A majority of Irish Catholics reject homophobia and respect LGBT+ persons. Government reports, such as Murphy, Ryan, etc. have sickened people and they have walked away. Adding to the distress, the Roman control brigade appears deaf and irreformable and living in a different world. Accordingly, moving away from clericalism and doing good elsewhere in God's presence is one sensible option for free persons. They are unlikely to return without evidence of significant progress. While such persons remain disillusioned and alienated from Catholicism, they are unlikely to enhance the religious instruction provided to their children in school.

I disagree with the suggestion that the Catholic Church should become smaller and reserved only for a conservative elite as a truly anti-modern group. I think the Gospel is for all people. The Catholic religion needs to be presented in new narrative, modern language and concepts, renewed ritual as well as updated structures. It is not possible to evangelise people today in the language of sexism, misogyny, patriarchy, monarchy, homophobia and exclusion. Elements of that language in the Catholic presentation are a hindrance to parents trying to transmit the faith.

There has been a lack of conversation, dialogue and honest communication among us Catholics. All aspects of worship, ritual and liturgical celebration require urgent review, improvement and updating. Massive reform of ministry, leadership and governance together with parish renewal is sorely needed. There must be greater emphasis on ecumenical cooperation to facilitate enriched faith encounter with Jesus Christ. A deficient and one-sided Church institution cannot convey joyful news of life to the full. A just, collegial and compassionate Church clearly working with the marginalised for justice and improved conditions will prove to be a beacon of hope.

Pope Francis asked for a "no" to abuse and clericalism. Those are nice words but we require a plan of action. We trust that the meetings with global bishops in February 2019 will be a start. Parish assemblies and diocesan synods over the coming years should gather together the good sense of the faithful. Vatican III needs to be convened as soon as possible.

I wish to thank you for your kind attention. I also enclose my Five Aims for Reform. Please bring my concerns and suggestions to the attention of the relevant authorities in Rome. I trust that you will enjoy your stay in Ireland and I pray that the Lord showers rich blessings on you in your ministry among us.

I am,

Yours faithfully,

_____

Joe Mulvaney

Enc 1

20

A PERSONAL CREDO

At the Church of the Sacred Heart and St Joseph, Rockfield, Coolaney, County Sligo

Maybe there will be no religion at all in a brave new world. Maybe people can live perfectly good lives without reference to God, religion, prayer, church or chapel. Maybe I am limited by my life experiences rooted in the 20th century. Maybe I am in thrall to programmed fears, worries or superstitions. Maybe I am entrapped in very limited categories. Maybe all of you in the 21st century will be liberated by technology into a totally different life experience or new reality. Those are all possibilities. However, in the meantime, I attempt to share the best of my Catholic religious understanding with you and hope it is of some benefit.

We all have different experiences and are initiated into different stories and groups. Some encounter caring people in the world and experience generosity, service and beauty. It is easy enough for those people to assert that all is good and that reality is gracious. Others encounter pain, illness, or persons who trespass against them. Their bad experience can have a very negative effect and it is understandable that such people could regard life as absurd or meaningless. Accordingly, there are many different viewpoints and stories about the world we share. People devise different solutions as to how to live bearably in time. There are many different religions and beliefs in a superhuman controlling power or personal god(s) who may provide meaning to life through revelation and relationship.

Great women and men have grappled over aeons as to the meaning of life. I would like to share two stories that I heard used many years ago in an attempt to explain and respect different religions. The first is that of the four blind men in contact with different parts of the body of an elephant. One blind man in contact only with a leg noted that the elephant is like a tree. Another, in contact with the trunk, proclaimed that the elephant is like a snake. They all defined and explained the elephant in different ways from limited perspectives. All were partly in the right; yet all were some way off from discerning the reality and full truth. Thus, there are many different religions and stories dealing with the mystery of Creation and the Meaning of Life. We can listen to all respectfully and raise questions. We can learn from all the partial truths and limited perspectives. We can run a mile from the religions that deal in hatred, supremacism, violence and exclusion. The acid test of good religious stories is whether they shelter and sustain. Do they help us encounter the divine depths in us and all creation? Do they produce – Love – Joy – Justice – Peace – Care for each other – Care for all of creation? The second story uses the example of a fly creeping up along a very large masterpiece painting in the National Gallery. That fly has a very limited perspective compared to our perspective as human beings at some distance back. In the same way, our human perspective about all of Creation may be quite limited.

History shows that Jesus lived two thousand years ago and emerged from the monotheistic Jewish religion. The Old Testament gives the earlier foundation stories and the New Testament provides different versions of his life, death and Resurrection. Believers in Jesus have assembled in communities or churches whose rituals, structures and systems have evolved over time. The creeds and documents of the various churches can be studied. The traditions and history of all the churches are there too for consideration by any person. Believers in Jesus or disciples of Jesus assert that there is meaning and purpose to all of the Universe beyond our limited comprehension and the obvious problems to do with pain, evil and physical death. Some Christians waged wars, crusades and persecution. However, over two thousand years there seemed to be a preponderance of loving service by billions of followers of Jesus.

I learned about Jesus within family and from neighbours, teachers, nuns and priests in a Roman Catholic parish community. A community or church of loving people doing service, healing and justice validates the basic message and the ongoing presence of a Creator/Saviour/Spirit of Love. Undoubtedly, there is some bad news and fake news all around us too. There are individuals in the world peddling lies and poison. There are groups prowling around seeking to destroy us with their theories of hatred and exclusion. We must be wary in our dealings with such people and seek to help them with our love, forgiveness and action. All of us are imperfect and are called to reflection, repentance, reform and development into fuller life. Family and parish community spoke to me about God the Creator. This God is close to us in the mystery of people, the wonder of creation and in personal prayer if we are mindful and have acquired the eyes to see. This God invites us to join in the dance of life and to contribute with the best of our talents in the ongoing task of creation and development.

Jesus called himself a Son of Man but related to God as his Father. Jesus experienced the divine depths within himself and explained that we are all daughters and sons of God. He taught that we are all loved by God and that we should respond with total love, joyful gratitude, selfless care for others and action for justice. His message of love, inclusion and care for all brought him to the attention of traditional religious authorities. He was confronted by Pharisees, hypocrites and hate groups peddling supremacism, exclusion, outdated traditions and cold, narrow legalism. He was clearly not orthodox and they threw him out to the civil authorities for crucifixion. Before his death, he invited his followers to a Passover meal. He suggested that they gather to share a meal in small groups in memory of him and to gain strength for their Exodus journey and their mission to feed the hungry. Jesus lived, loved, suffered, died and rose again to a new dimension of life. Sometime after his death, his disciples experienced the Risen Christ among them. We are all invited along the same pilgrim way with him to build up the Kingdom of God or the new creation. My faith journey has taught me that while we are all crossed by sin, sickness, pain and death, we are all called to encounter healing and life to the full with the Risen Christ Jesus made manifest to us in the loving presence and actions of family and a caring community of women and men.

I also learned about the Holy Spirit of Wisdom and Love from within my community. The first disciples of Jesus were bewildered and frightened. However, we are told that they experienced a powerful Spirit of God enabling them to proclaim the ongoing presence of Jesus Christ and sending them forth to share, care, heal and celebrate life to the full. That enterprise forged ahead over two thousand years and we are invited to call that Holy Spirit of God into our lives in the 21st century. That same Holy Spirit is available to us all together as a community to devise new language and narrative about God. We were taught that the same Holy Spirit of Wisdom is available to guide us in our relationships, parenting, family enrichment and work in the public realm for justice and the common good.

I believe that the Revelation of God did not stop two thousand years ago. A loving God is clearly revealed in the care and service provided by good people and sincere believers. God's Word to us is not confined to any old books, folk tales or ancient stories. The Risen Lord is with us as we gather in his name. God is with us everywhere in our world and will deliver us from evil with the cooperation of people and communities. The Holy Spirit of God leads us on our Exodus journey out of ignorance, slavery, oppression and injustice. God speaks to us today in the best of modern, human knowledge, insight, songs, music and art. The documents of Vatican II advanced the Revelation of God. God's Word comes to us from females and males and all of creation. However, it appears to me that Word of God for the future may come to us in small basic communities engaged in reflection, prayer, study, dialogue, sharing of wholesome life experience and action for justice.

The Church or the community of disciples of Jesus has come to assert that life is changed but not ended at death and that there are many new dimensions risen beyond our limited horizons. The community invites all to experience growth, healing and life to the full with the Risen Christ. All are assured that God is Love and that each individual is loved as a special person. All are invited to respond with love for God and neighbour. All are challenged to avoid trespass, feed the hungry and act for justice. Continue your search for God or a Saviour or a Spirit of Meaning and Purpose. Get to know the Jesus of the Gospels and walk with the Risen Lord together with other Christians. Do good, work for justice and help to build a better world. Count your blessings and give thanks.

All of the above is expressed in traditional Catholic concepts. Our spiritual or religious needs can also be expressed in the neutral language regarding a Higher Power. We all need to relate in some way to a Higher Power in our lives. We all need updated, healthy, modern religion or spirituality in our lives. We marvel at the daily order in the Universe and the wonder of sun, moon, stars, galaxies and space. We experience our human powers and encounter wonderful people and experiences. We all then need to hand over everything to the Higher Power of the Universe as we journey in wonder and, especially, when we experience our frailty, fears and needs.

We all need to slow down, stop, breathe deeply, be mindful and hand over to the Higher Power in the secrecy of our own private space. The next step is to come out of our isolation in boxes or smartphones or cyberspace. We all need to experience the riches of family or community and to do good together. We all need to talk, share, listen and dialogue as we support each other in various kinds of small groups. Together, we can imagine and build a better world.

We all need to develop our moral compass in line with the best of human insight today and our personal connection with the Higher Power. We all need to be fully alive and joyful in positive, constructive ways. On the principle that love is all you need, we can develop our relationships and work for peace. Feeding the hungry, housing the homeless, working for justice and caring for the environment will bring joy and fulfilment.

We are all on the road together to God knows where as we watch Voyager II disappear into interstellar space. We are content to travel along with Jesus Christ – the Lord of the Dance – as he invites us out of our selfish preoccupation towards fuller and more satisfying life. We will continue singing our song and doing good. We will heal and help and build. We will continue to speak out for justice and reform. We will act as if all depends on us and we will pray as if all depends on God. We don't know what is around the corner and there are no guarantees. We have been through much change in the course of our life here below. What lies beyond is another dimension or nothing. No one knows for sure. There is only silence from beyond the moon and the graveyards can be bleak. The Bible says that "eye hath not seen nor ear heard what God has prepared for those who love him." The funeral liturgy contains a comforting phrase, "Life is changed, not ended." I continue to have faith and believe in the Good News of Jesus Christ. The Christian story sustained our families and forebears. It provided shelter for them and helped them to live bearably in time. It has helped me. It can do the same for you and yours into the future if it is updated, reformulated and restructured. The Jesus story has to be in your language. That is what I hope to help achieve by this book. May the Lord bless us all along the way and the Higher Power be our stronghold.

EPILOGUE

Pope Francis has returned to Rome with our prayers for his good health and wellbeing. We know he faces entrenched opposition from a small group of traditionalists. The burdens and expectations are indeed huge and probably excessive for an elderly man. He needs a powerful collegial team of men and women around him to give wise advice and support at this time of crisis. He received a warm welcome from officialdom together with hundreds of thousands of Irish people. As confirmation that local edicts can change, he told survivor mothers that it was not a mortal sin for them to seek out their children stolen from them. Various people spoke their truth very clearly to him. I pray that he will have the strength and ability to initiate the required actions after lovely words, multiple expressions of sorrow and nice gestures. His planned summit at the Vatican in February 2019 is a good step along the road. I hope that he will be able to inspire the bishops everywhere to join in a plan of action drilling down to the roots of the crisis within clericalism. A disordered and dysfunctional Church institution which excludes women will inevitably produce abuse by predators and official cover-up. Catholics who accept the above diagnosis have a huge challenge to convert the hierarchy who still don't get it or who have not the slightest intention of proceeding with significant reform. It is right that we evangelise the hierarchy and work with them for change.

There are serious questions to be answered by the hierarchy in the Catholic Church and there are also questions for us as lay people. Media reports have raised further questions about the willingness of some bishops to cooperate in serious safeguarding action as recommended by lay experts. Are the bishops in every country prepared to confront the root causes buried within a clerical meaning system and ethos? Serious questions have been posed to

Pope Francis and some cardinals concerning their knowledge of sexual deviance and their complicity in the Canon Law regime of cover-up. Will the Vatican continue to refuse cooperation with legitimate State authorities investigating crimes against children? Will the Holy See continue to claim immunity? Is it all a charade to blame bishops who acted as obedient members of a club? How should lay Catholics respond to the small group of clerics and traditionalists who continue to thwart updating and reform? Have lay people any chance in an ecclesial institution where some shepherds have preyed on the flock and given the attitudes of some bishops as revealed in the Pennsylvania Report? Are too many devout lay Catholics turning a blind eye out of religious loyalty or fear? How can we avoid collusion with an unreformed Curia and disassociate ourselves from clericalism?

I am placing much hope on the hugely important Letter of His Holiness Pope Francis to the People of God. He stated that there must be active participation by all Catholics in the much-needed ecclesial and social change. He stated that we must do so in a real way by playing an equal role in a program of reform within the Catholic Church. He said that no effort must be spared to create a new culture to prevent and eliminate abuse and official cover-up. Presuming that the Roman control brigade does not stifle the papal project, I take it to mean that this will involve women and men sharing in teaching, service, ministry and governance. If all this is implemented, it will indeed be a revolution and will usher in a new Catholic Church era of truth, justice and love.

So far, nothing has changed. We have had a surfeit of nice words, symbols and gestures. Now, we all need the hierarchy to join with us in the work of reform and it is time to take action.

BIBLIOGRAPHY

Abbott, Walter SJ, and Gallagher, Joseph Very Rev. *The Documents of Vatican II: The Message and Meaning of the Ecumenical Council.* London/Dublin: Geoffrey Chapman, 1966

Alinsky, Saul D. *Rules for Radicals: A Practical Primer for Realistic Radicals.* New York: Vintage Books, 1972

Beattie, Tina. *Woman, New Century Theology.* New York/London: Continuum, 2003

Berry, Joseph. *Render unto Rome: The Secret Life of Money in the Roman Catholic Church.* New York: Broadway Paperbacks, 2011

Bianchi, Eugene, and Ruether, Rosemary (editors). *A Democratic Catholic Church: The Reconstruction of Roman Catholicism.* New York: Crossroad, 1992

Brydon-Brook, Simon. *Take, Bless, Break, Share: Agapes, Table Blessings and Liturgies.* Norwich: Canterbury Press, 1998 (An agape is a love feast held by early Christians in connection with the Lord's Supper. This small book gives a selection of simple prayers for the use of small groups gathered in the name of Jesus)

Buckley, Bishop Pat. *A Sexual Life, A Spiritual Life: A Painful Journey to Inner Peace.* Dublin: The Liffey Press, 2005

Byrne, Lavinia. *Woman at the Altar: Ordination of Women in the Roman Catholic Church.* London: Mowbray, 1994

Carroll, James. *Practising Catholic.* Boston: Mariner Books, 2009

Carter, Jimmy (former US President). *A Call to Action: Women, Religion, Violence and Power.* New York: Simon and Schuster, 2014 (In a review of this book in the National Catholic Reporter of December 5-18, 2014, Janice Sevre-Duszynska, a Roman catholic woman priest, wrote as follows "if the Roman Catholic Church declared the full equality of women and women's voices, that teaching would echo through the wounded patriarchal cultures of the world")

Chittister, Joan Sr. OSB. *Woman Strength: Modern Church, Modern Woman.* New York: Sheed & Ward, 1990

Collins, Paul. *Papal Power: A Proposal for Change in Catholicism's Third Millennium*. Blackburn, Victoria: Harper Collins Religious, 1997

Collins, Paul. *Seven Prominent Catholics and Their Struggle with the Vatican*. London: Continuum, 2001

Cozzens, Donald. *The Changing Face of the Priesthood*. Collegeville, Minnesota: Liturgical Press, 2000

Cozzens, Donald. *Sacred Silence: Denial and the Crisis in the Church*. Collegeville, Minnesota: Liturgical Press, 2004

Crosby, Michael. *The Dysfunctional Church: Addiction and Codependency in the Family of Catholicism*. Notre Dame, Indiana: Ave Maria Press, 1991

Daly, Gabriel OSA. *The Church Always in Need of Reform*. Dublin: Dominican Publications, 2015

Davis, Charles. *A Question of Conscience*. London: Hodder & Stoughton, 1967

De Chardin, Pierre Teilhard S.J. *Milieu Divin: An Essay On the Interior Life*. Various editions.

Deegan, Eileen Sr C.S.B. *Parish Rituals for Key Moments*. Dublin: Columba Press, 2005 (This book is very useful for lay ministers. Many Catholics today walk with God in their own way but are turned off from current parish liturgies and devotions. The rituals in this book are an attempt to reach such people and touch into key moments in their lives).

Delio, Ilia. *The Emergent Christ: Exploring the Meaning of Catholic in an Evolutionary Universe*. Maryknoll, New York: Orbis Books, 2011

Delio, Ilia. *Making All Things New: Catholicity, Cosmology, Consciousness*. Maryknoll, New York: Orbis Books, 2015

De Rosa, Peter. *Vicars of Christ: The Dark Side of the Papacy*. London: Corgi Books, 1989

Devlin, Patricia, and Glennon, Brian. *To Have and to Hold: Stories and Reflections from LGBT People, their Families and Friends*. Published by the Authors, 2015 tohaveandtoholdlgbt@gmail.com, 2015

Dorr, Donal. *Time for a Change: A Fresh Look at Spirituality, Sexuality, Globalisation and the Church*. Dublin: Columba Press, 2004

Dorr, Donal. *The Pope Francis Agenda*. Dublin: Veritas, 2018

Doyle, Thomas et al. *Sex, Priests and Secret Codes: The Catholic Church's 2000 Year Paper Trail of Sexual Abuse*. Los Angeles: Volt Press, 2006

Dunn, Joseph. *No Lions in the Hierarchy*. Dublin: Columba Press, 1994

Fagan, Sean SM. *Does Morality Change?* Dublin: Columba Press, 2003

Fagan, Sean SM. *What Happened to Sin?* Dublin: Columba Press, 2008

Farley, Margaret. *A Framework for Christian Sexual Ethics.* New
York/London: Continuum, 2006

Fiedler, Maureen and Rabben, Linda (editors). *Rome Has Spoken. A Guide to
Forgotten Papal Statements, and How They Have Changed Through the
Centuries.* New York: Crossroad, 1998

Flannery, Austin OP. *Vatican Council II, Vol I, Conciliar and Post Conciliar
Documents.* Dublin: Dominican Publications, 1998

Flannery, Tony. *Keeping the Faith: Church of Rome or Church of Christ.* Cork:
Mercier Press, 2005

Flannery, Tony (editor). *Responding to the Ryan Report.* Dublin: Columba
Press, 2009

Flannery, Tony. *A Question of Conscience.* Dublin: Londubh Books, 2013

Fox, Matthew. *Original Blessing: A Primer in Creation Spirituality.* Rochester,
Vermont: Bear & Company, 1983

Francis I. *Evangelii Gaudium: The Joy of the Gospel.* Dublin: Veritas, 2013

Francis I. *Laudato Si: On Care for our Common Home.* Dublin: Veritas, 2015

Francis I. *Amoris Laetitia: On Love in the Family.* Dublin: Veritas, 2016

Francis I. *Gaudete et Exsultate: On the Call to Holiness in Today's World.*
Dublin: Veritas, 2018

Frankl, Viktor. *Man's Search for Meaning.* London: Rider, 2004

Gaillardetz, Richard and Clifford, Catherine. *Keys to the Council: Unlocking
the Teaching of Vatican II.* Collegeville, Minnesota: Liturgical Press, 2012

Greeley, Andrew. *Priests in the United States: Reflections on a Survey.* New
York: Doubleday, 1972

Hanley, Angela, and Smyth, David (editors). *Quench not the Spirit: Theology
and Prophecy in the Modern World.* Dublin: Columba Press, 2005

Hanley, Angela. *Whose A La Carte Menu? Exploring Catholic Themes in
Context.* Dublin: Columba Press, 2014

Harrington, Donal. *Christianity at its Best.* Dublin: Columba Press, 2012

Harrington, Donal. *Tomorrow's Parish.* Dublin: Columba Press, 2018

Higgins, Cathy. *Churches in Exile: Alternative Models of Church for Ireland in
the 21st Century.* Dublin: Columba Press, 2013

Hoban, Brendan. *Pieces of my Mind.* Dublin: Banley House, 2007

Hoban, Brendan. *Change or Decay: Irish Catholicism in Crisis*. Dublin: Banley House

Huebsch, Bill with Thurmes, Paul. *Vatican II in Plain English* (Three Volumes). Allen, Texas: Thomas More, 1996

John Paul II. *Catechism of the Catholic Church*. Dublin: Veritas, 1994

Johnson, Elizabeth. *She Who Is: The Mystery of God in Feminist Theological Discourse*. New York: Crossroad, 1992 & 2002

Johnson, Elizabeth. *Quest for the Living God: Mapping Frontiers in the Theology of God*. New York/London: Continuum, 2007

Jung, Carl Gustav. *Modern Man in Search of a Soul*. London: Routledge Classics, 2001

Kaiser, Robert Blair. *The Encyclical That Never Was*. London: Sheed & Ward, 1987

Kaufman, Philip OSB. *Why You Can Disagree and Remain a Faithful Catholic*. New York: Crossroad, 1989

Keenan, Marie. *Child Sexual Abuse and the Catholic Church: Gender, Power and Organizational Culture*. New York: Oxford University Press, 2012 (This book raises very serious questions as to whether sexual abuse is inevitable given the meaning system that is taught by the official Catholic Church and to which many priests adhere)

Kennerley, Ginnie. *Embracing Women: Making History in the Church of Ireland*. Dublin: Columba Press, 2008

Kowalski, Anthony. *Married Catholic Priests: Their History, Their Journeys, Their Reflections*. New York: Crossroad, 2004

Küng, Hans. *Truthfulness: The Future of the Church*. London: Sheed & Ward, 1968

Küng, Hans. *On Being a Christian*. London: Collins, 1977

Küng, Hans. *Can We Save the Catholic Church? We Can Save the Catholic Church!* London: William Collins, 2013

Küng, Hans. *The Catholic Church: A Short History*. Trans. John Bowden. New York: Modern Library, 2003

Malone, Mary T. *Women and Christianity: Volume 1: The First Thousand Years*. Dublin: Columba Press, 2000

Malone, Mary T. *Women and Christianity: Volume 2: The Medieval Period AD 1000-1500*. Dublin: Columba Press, 2001

Malone, Mary T. *Women and Christianity: Volume 3: From the Reformation to the 21st Century*. Dublin: Columba Press, 2003

Malone, Mary T. *The Elephant in the Church: A Woman's Tract for our Times*. Dublin: Columba Press, 2014

Martin, James S.J. *The Jesuit Guide to (almost) Everything: A Spirituality for Real Life*. New York: Harper One, 2010

Martin, James S.J. *Building a Bridge: How the Catholic Church and LGBT Community Can Enter into a Relationship of Respect, Compassion and Sensitivity*. New York: Harper One, 2018

McAleese, Mary. *Quo Vadis? Collegiality in the Code of Canon Law*. Dublin: Columba Press, 2012

McBrien, Richard P. *Catholicism*. London: Geoffrey Chapman, 1981

McCarthy, Eamonn. *Now is The Time: A Celebration of Women's Call to a Renewed Priesthood in the Catholic Church. First International Conference – Text and Context*. BASIC, 2002

McClory, Robert. *Turning Point: The Inside Story of the Papal Birth Control Commission and How Humanae Vitae Changed the Life of Patty Crowley and the Future of the Church*. New York: Crossroad, 1995

McDonagh, Sean. *Climate Change: The Challenge to All of Us*. Columba Press, 2007

McDonagh, Sean. *Laudato Si: An Irish Response*. Veritas, 2018

McGillicuddy, Mary. *John Moriarty: Not The Whole Story*. The Lilliput Press, 2018

McKenzie, John L S.J. *Authority in the Church*. London: Geoffrey Chapman, 1966

McNeill, John J. *The Church and the Homosexual*. Boston: Beacon Press, 1993

McNeill, John J. *Taking a Chance on God: Liberating Theology for Gays, Lesbians, and Their Lovers, Families, and Friends*. Boston: Beacon Press, 1996

McVeigh, Joe. *Renewing the Irish Church: Towards an Irish Liberation Theology*. Cork: Mercier Press, 1993

Meehan, Bridget-Mary (editor), McGrath, Elsie (editor), Raming, Ida (editor). *Women Find A Way: The Movement And Stories Of Roman Catholic Women Priests*. College Station, Texas: Virtual Bookworm Publishing, 2008

Meehan, Bridget-Mary. *The Healing Power of Prayer: New Expanded Edition.* Create Space Independent Publishing Platform, 2017

Moriarty, John. *Serious Sounds.* Sli na Firinne Publishing, 2006

Morwood, Michael MSC. *Tomorrow's Catholic: Understanding God and Jesus in a New Millennium.* New London, Connecticut: Twenty Third Publications, 1997

Murphy, Claire SHCJ. *Woman as Church: The Challenge to Change.* Dublin: Gill & MacMillan, 1997

Nolan, Albert. *Jesus Before Christianity.* Maryknoll, New York: Orbis Books, 1992

Nolan, Albert. *Jesus Today: A Spirituality of Radical Freedom.* Maryknoll, New York: Orbis Books, 2006

O'Brien, David J, and Shannon, Thomas A. *Catholic Social Thought: Encyclicals and Documents from Pope Leo XIII to Pope Francis.* Maryknoll, New York: Orbis Books, 2017

O'Connor, Dagmar. *How to make love to the same person for the rest of your life and still love it.* London: Columbus Books, 1985

O'Donohue, John. *Anam Cara: Spiritual Wisdom from the Celtic World.* London: Bantam Press, 1997

O'Donohue, John (in conversation with John Quinn). *Walking on the Pastures of Wonder.* Dublin: Veritas, 2015

O'Halloran, James SDB. *Living Cells: Vision and Practicalities of Small Christian Communities and Groups.* Dublin: Columba Press, 2011

O'Halloran, James SDB. *In Search of Christ: A Prayer Book for Seekers.* Dublin: Columba Press, 2004

O'Halloran, James SDB. *The Brendan Book of Prayer – for small groups.* Dublin: Columba Press, 2003

O'Hanlon, Gerry SJ. *A New Vision for the Catholic Church – A View from Ireland.* Dublin: Columba Press, 2011

O'Hanlon, Gerry SJ. *The Quiet Revolution of Pope Francis: A Synodal Catholic Church in Ireland.* Dublin: Messenger Publications, 2018

O'Mahony, T. P. *Why the Catholic Church Needs Vatican III.* Dublin: Columba Press, 2010

O'Malley, John W. *What Happened at Vatican II.* Cambridge, Massachusetts: Belknap Press of Harvard University Press, 2008.

O'Murchu, Diarmuid. *Religion in Exile: A Spiritual Vision for the Homeward Bound*. Dublin: Gateway, 2000

Pagola, José. *Jesus: An Historical Approximation*. Trans. Margaret Wild. Miami, Florida: Convivium Press, 2009

Raab, Kelley A. *When Women Become Priests*. New York: Columbia University Press, 2000

Ranke-Heinemann, Uta. *Eunuchs for the Kingdom of Heaven: Women, Sexuality and the Catholic Church*. Trans. Peter Heinegg. New York: Penguin Books, 1990

Rice, David. *Shattered Vows: Exodus from the Priesthood*. London: Michael Joseph, 1990

Robertson, Geoffrey Q.C. *The Case of the Pope: Vatican Accountability for Human Rights Abuse*. London: Penguin Books, 2010

Robinson, Bishop Geoffrey. *Confronting Power and Sex in the Catholic Church: Reclaiming the Spirit of Jesus*. Dublin: Columba Press, 2007

Rowland, Clare (ed). *Women Sharing Fully in the Ministry of Christ*. Dublin: Dublin: Blackwater Press, 1995

Ruether, Rosemary Radford. *Womenguides: Readings Towards a Feminist Theology*. Boston: Beacon Press, 1985

Salzmann, Todd and Lawler, Michael. *The Sexual Person: Towards a Renewed Catholic Anthropology*. Washington DC: Georgetown University Press, 2008

Schillebeeckx, Edward. *Ministry: A Case for Change*. Trans. John Bowden. London: SCM Press Ltd, 1980

Shenck, Christine C.S.J. *Crispina And Her Sisters: Women And Authority in Early Christianity*. Fortress Press, 2017

Simon, William E Jr. *Great Catholic Parishes: How Four Essential Practices Make Them Thrive*. Notre Dame, Indiana: Ave Maria Press, 2016

Sipe, A.W. Richard. *Sex, Priests and Power: Anatomy of a Crisis*. London: Cassell, 1995

Sipe, A.W. Richard. *A Secret World: Sexuality And The Search For Celibacy*. Routledge, 2013

Swimme, Brian, and Berry, Thomas. *The Universe Story*. San Francisco: Harper, 1992 (The above two authors together with Ilia Delio, Michael Morwood, Diarmuid O'Murchu and Matthew Fox among others, appear to be exploring the hugely important area of new narrative or new presentation of the Good News of Jesus Christ in this 21ˢᵗ century)

Tighe-Mooney, Sharon. *What About Me? Women and the Catholic Church.* Cork, Mercier Press, 2018

Wijngaards, John. *The Ordination of Women in the Catholic Church: Unmasking a Cuckoo's Egg Tradition.* London: Darton Longman & Todd, 2001

Winter, Miriam Therese. *Out of the Depths: The Story of Ludmila Javorova, Ordained Roman Catholic Priest.* New York: Crossroad Publishing Company, 2001

Zagano, Phyllis. *Women in Ministry: Emerging Questions about the Diaconate.* New Jersey: Paulist Press, 2012

Recommended Websites

wearechurchireland.ie	We Are Church Ireland
womenpriests.org	Arguments for and against women priests
theolibrary.shc.edu	Spring Hill College in Mobile, Alabama (USA)
ncronline.org	National Catholic Reporter (USA)
associationofcatholicpriests.ie	Association of Catholic Priests in Ireland
we-are-church.org	We Are Church International
acireland.ie	Association of Catholics in Ireland
womensordinationcampaign.org	Women's Ordination Worldwide
thetablet.co.uk	The Tablet (UK)
thebodyissacred.org	The Catholic Church and Sexuality
thepeoplespeakout.org	
wesupportpopefrancis.net	
catholicchurchreform.org	
acalltoaction.org.uk	
solasbhride.ie	An initiative of the Brigidine Sisters in Kildare. Invites people to walk in the footsteps of St Brigid. It provides a quiet space for prayer and reflection, with conference and meeting rooms also available.
arcwp.org	Association of Roman Catholic Women Priests
mariecollins.net	
bridgetmarys.blogspot.com	

"Working to end injustices in the Roman Catholic Church."

Members of the We Are Church International Movement (IMWAC)
Members of Women's Ordination Worldwide (WOW)

    f   We Are Church Ireland
    E: info@wearechurchireland.ie
    W: www.wearechurchireland.ie

What is We Are Church? Take note again of the huge change in Vatican II which stated that Church is the People of God rather than a clerical group. It also stated that we are all baptised into the mission of Christ rather than just being allowed the lowest levels of a clerical operation. So, all of us, as baptised persons have special talents and We Are Church!

We Are Church started in Austria in 1995 when a group of concerned Catholics (lay and ordained) set up a process to discover the wishes of the people for the future of their Church. Those hopes found expression in the form of a petition. This initiative spread quickly to Germany and before long, 2.3 million signatures had been collected. During the months that followed many other countries in Europe, the US, South America, Africa, Australia joined the process and this development led to the formation of the International Movement We Are Church (IMWAC) in 1996.

Those petitions that gave expression to the longing of many Catholics for real and lasting reform in the Church were presented to Rome in October 1997.

We Are Church, Ireland, was set up in 1997 by a group of women and men concerned about the direction of the Catholic Church in Ireland.

Remaining faithful to our own baptismal vows and to the spirit of Vatican II, and in common with the International Movement of We Are Church, We Are Church Ireland, has produced a set of Five Aims in prayerful hope for the necessary urgent reform and renewal within the Church which we all love.

The Five Aims/Objectives are:

1. Equality of all the baptised where decision making is actively shared by all, with appropriate structures for this.
2. Full participation of women in all aspects of church life, including priesthood.
3. Recognition of the primacy of an informed conscience.
4. Promotion of a positive attitude towards sexuality and the removal of the obligation of clerical celibacy.
5. An inclusive church, open and welcoming to all, which does not marginalise people because of their sexual orientation, marital status or for any other reason.

The website wearechurchireland.ie gives more details. If you agree with the Five Aims, I encourage you to become a member of We Are Church. The annual subscription is only €10 or €5 (if you are unwaged or aged over 65). You will find an application form on the wearechurchireland.ie website or just send an email. I also encourage you to form a We Are Church group in your parish for debate, dialogue, further education, prayer and action to end injustices in our Catholic Church. I encourage you and your group to continue to lobby for reform on an ongoing basis as well as sending off the letters proposed in this project to the Papal Nuncio, bishops and your parish priest. Please contact us via the website and Facebook page. We will be glad to acknowledge your existence as a local group in case other people in your area wish to join and share support. We will be delighted to receive any new ideas or creative suggestions you may have to further the work of justice and reform.

APPENDIX B – DIOCESAN CONTACT INFORMATION

Achonry
Awaiting appointment of Bishop
Edmondstown, Ballaghaderreen, Co. Roscommon
Email: bishop@achonrydiocese.org

Ardagh
and Clonmacnoise
Bishop Francis Duffy
St Michael's, Longford, Co. Longford
Email: ardaghdi@iol.ie

Armagh
Archbishop Eamon Martin
Ara Coeli, Armagh BT61 7QY
Email: admin@aracoeli.com

Cashel and Emly
Archbishop Kieran O'Reilly
Archbishop's House, Thurles, Co. Tipperary
Email: office@cashel-emly.ie

Clogher
Awaiting appointment of Bishop
Oifig an Easpaig, Monaghan
Email: diocesanoffice@clogherdiocese.ie

Clonfert
Bishop John Kirby
Coorheen, Loughrea, Co. Galway
Email: clonfert@iol.ie

Cloyne
Bishop William Crean
Cloyne Diocesan Centre, Cobh, Co. Cork
Email: info@cloynediocese.ie

Cork and Ross
Bishop John Buckley
Diocesan Offices, Redemption Road, Cork
Email: secretary@corkandross.org

Derry
Bishop Donal McKeown
PO Box 227, Bishop's House, Derry, BT48 9YG
Email: office@derrydiocese.org

Down and Connor
Bishop Noël Treanor
73 Somerton Road, Belfast, Co. Antrim BT15 4DE
Email: dcoffice@downandconnor.org

Dromore
Bishop Philip Boyce (Administrator)
44 Armagh Rd, Newry, Co. Down BT35 6PN
Email: bishopofdromore@btinternet.com

Dublin	Archbishop Diarmuid Martin Archbishop's House, Drumcondra, Dublin 9 Email: info@dublindiocese.ie
	Bishop Raymond Field 3 Castleknock Road, Blanchardstown, Dublin 15
	Bishop Eamonn Walsh Naomh Brid, Blessington Road, Tallaght, Dublin 24
Elphin	Bishop Kevin Doran Diocesan Office, St Mary's, Temple Street, Sligo Email: office@elphindiocese.ie
Ferns	Bishop Denis Brennan Bishop's House, Summerhill, Wexford Email: adm@ferns.ie
Galway, Kilmacduagh & Kilfenora	Bishop Brendan Kelly Mount St Mary's, Taylor's Hill, Galway Email: galwaydiocese@eircom.net
Kerry	Bishop Raymond Browne Bishop's House, Killarney, Co. Kerry Email: bishopshouse@eircom.net
Kildare and Leighlin	Bishop Denis Nulty Bishop's House, Old Dublin Road, Carlow Email: bishop@kandle.ie
Killala	Bishop John Fleming Bishop's House, Ballina, Co. Mayo Email: deocilala@eircom.net
Killaloe	Bishop Fintan Monahan Westbourne, Ennis, Co. Clare Email: office@killaloediocese.ie
Kilmore	Bishop Philip Leo O'Reilly Bishop's House, Cullies, Co. Cavan Email: bishop@kilmorediocese.ie
Limerick	Bishop Brendan Leahy Social Service Centre, Henry Street, Limerick Email: office@ldo.ie

Meath	Bishop Thomas Deenihan Bishop's House, Dublin Rd, Mullingar, Westmeath Email: bishop@dioceseofmeath.ie
Ossory	Bishop Dermot Farrell Blessed Felix House, Tilbury Place, Kilkenny Email: bishop@ossory.ie
Raphoe	Bishop Alan McGuckian Ard Adhamhnáin, Letterkenny, Co. Donegal Email: raphoediocese@eircom.net
Tuam	Archbishop Michael Neary Archbishop's House, Tuam, Co. Galway Email: admin@tuamarchdiocese.org
Waterford and Lismore	Bishop Alphonsus Cullinan Bishop's House, John's Hill, Waterford Email: waterfordlismore@eircom.net

Other Contact Points:

Irish Catholic Bishops Conference	Columba Centre, Maynooth, Co. Kildare
The Papal Nuncio	Archbishop Jude Thaddeus Okolo Apostolic Nunciature, 183 Navan Road, Dublin 7 Email: nuncioirl@eircom.net